Webster's New World™
POWER VOCABULARY

Elizabeth Morse-Cluley
Richard Read

Prentice Hall
New York • London • Toronto • Sydney • Tokyo • Singapore

First Edition

 Prentice Hall General Reference
15 Columbus Circle
New York, NY 10023

A Webster's New World™ Book

Webster's New World Dictionary and colophon are
registered trademarks of Simon & Schuster, Inc.
Prentice Hall is a registered trademark of Prentice-Hall, Inc.

Library of Congress Cataloging-in-Publication Data

Morse-Cluley, Elizabeth.
     Webster's New World power vocabulary
      1. Vocabulary I. Read, Richard. II. Title
PE1449.M68 1988   428.1   88-17147
ISBN 0-671-79998-3

Manufactured in the United States of America

5 6 7 8 9 10

Contents

INTRODUCTION

Improve Your Command of the Language

The power of your vocabulary—whether spoken or written—is a deciding factor in your success, and if your goal is to succeed, then this book was written for you.

Professional studies and reports show the critical relationship between success and command of the language. There is evidence that the only common characteristic of successful people in all fields in the United States is an exceptionally good grasp of word meanings. The best executives, regardless of their level of formal education, invariably score highest on word tests. Indeed, every kind of standardized test—psychological, scholastic, aptitude, civil service—leans heavily on vocabulary as a measure of ability.

It would appear, then, that if you build up your powers of expression, you will help yourself to get ahead, simply because words are the tools of thought. They can help you grasp the thoughts of others and communicate your own ideas more clearly and effectively.

It doesn't matter what your command of vocabulary is now. You can improve it with the help of this book. Read it, absorb it, and test yourself with the many word challenges it contains. The words included here are the words used over and over again by successful, articulate people and the ones that will have the greatest effect on your own powers of expression.

Building Your Powers of Expression

The major objective of this book is to show you how to close the gap between your *functional* vocabulary (those words you use regularly and comfortably) and your *recognition* vocabulary (those words you are aware of to some extent but do not use). Following the step-by-step approach of this book, you can easily double—or triple—your functional vocabulary.

Here's how it works:

- *Part I* focuses on the building blocks of English words—the foundation of a power vocabulary.
- *Part II* presents the interesting effects of borrowed words, evolved and invented words, foreign terms and specialized vocabularies.

1

- *Part III* highlights the troublesome oddities of English such as spelling, plural forms, compound words and "problem pairs."
- *Part IV* provides a thousand powerful words that should be part of your vocabulary.
- *Part V* includes master word challenges to measure your mastery of the power words you have learned.

An Overview: The Power of The English Language

Nothing is more frustrating than learning something without knowing the how's and why's. Real learning requires a solid understanding of how something happened or why something is done in a certain way. If your goal is to increase your vocabulary power, then you'll need to know the basic how's and why's of the English language.

The English language has more words than any other language—by some estimates, close to two million! It also has more sets of *synonyms* (words with the same or similar meanings) and *antonyms* (words with opposite meaning) than any other language. How did this happen? you might ask. Why is it important to me? How will this affect my ability to build a power vocabulary?

If we answer the first question, we'll automatically answer the others. Unlike other languages, English is a hybrid tongue, a colorful mixture of words formed or borrowed throughout the years. The reason for the unique richness of English is its essentially dual nature: Latinate and Germanic.

Originally, English was a Germanic language spoken by the Anglo-Saxon peoples in the British Isles. They were later invaded by the Norman-French who spoke a Latin-based Romance tongue. Over the years, these two very different languages intermingled to produce a completely new language and grammar composed of bits and pieces from both.

This explains why "traditional" English grammar is so full of exceptions, contradictions, and confusing rules. What the traditional grammar tries to do is explain how a Germanic language works according to Latinate rules.

Similar inconsistencies appear in English vocabulary, too. If a word was weak or missing in Anglo-Saxon, and the French had a better word for the concept, we borrowed theirs. Or, if we needed additional words to explain finer distinctions of meaning, we kept the original word for certain occasions and used the new synonym for others. For example, the simple Germanic word for an average person's home is *house*. But the home of a rich man is a *mansion* (French) and the home of a huge institution or organization is an *edifice* (Latin). They all mean *dwelling* or *building*, but they reflect subtle differences in *connotation* (the emotional effect of a word beyond the literal meaning) and *level of language* (the formality or informality of vocabulary chosen on different occasions). Knowing this important characteristic of the English language can help you improve your command of the language.

The common, everyday language we speak is overwhelmingly Germanic in origin. As our environment becomes more formal, sophisticated, or technical, so too must our vocabulary. And the words we choose in these settings are predominantly Romance-, Latin-, or Greek-based words.

Many of the Romance-based words we use have been absorbed unchanged into our everyday speech—*gauche* or *avant garde*, for example. We often use these words when we talk about the particular subject areas from which we borrowed them. For example, most of our vocabulary describing the arts and music comes straight from the Italian (*chiaroscuro, coloratura*), that describing cooking and fashion from the French (*souffle, chemise*).

The most significant portion, however, of our higher-level words—close to 70%—comes to us from Latin and Greek. These ancient tongues provide us with the many prefixes, root elements, and suffixes needed in a modern technological society. Because these Latin and Greek word elements are the basis of a power vocabulary, they are the focus of this book. Yet this book takes a completely new approach to vocabulary building. It does not aim to make you a master of trivia or obscure terms. Rather, it presents "old" material in a new way. It shows you how to build upon word elements by "clustering," and it gives you the how's and why's of building a power vocabulary in digestible, self-paced sections.

Strategies for Building Your Vocabulary

You can take several steps immediately to improve your vocabulary power. The simplest, of course, is to *listen carefully to people who express themselves well.* Notice how they always choose the perfect word. Notice how they say much in few words. These two talents are flip sides of the same coin. By using the most precise word to express a concept, these people avoid vague, rambling, and imprecise statements. They use strong, precise verbs (*captivates*) instead of weak, muddy phrases (*is captivated by*). They have a solid understanding of the connotative differences among synonyms and can thus project far more meaning in one carefully chosen word than can careless or fuzzy thinkers.

You may be thinking that you've never needed such fine-tuned word choices. But until you realize how many subtle word choices you have at your disposal, you'll never recognize the instances when you *do* need them. For example, a young child doesn't "need" the word *democracy*. Later on, though, the grown-up child will see the need for a precise word to express the concept "rule of the people" and its many connotations. And so, knowing the Greek word elements *demo* (people) and *cracy* (rule), this person will understand the precise structure and meaning of the word *democracy*.

Another example: Using the word "pagan" might be sufficient for expressing a general idea to a general audience. But if you were speaking to a sophisticated audience, say, members of the clergy, you would want to be much more precise. Are you referring to someone who does not believe in God—an atheist (Greek: *a-* "not," *theo-* "God," *-ist* "one who")—or are you describing someone who isn't sure whether God exists or not—an agnostic (Greek: *a-* "not," *gnos-* "knowledge," *-tic* "one who")? A fine distinction, true, but a very important one.

Understanding Words in Context

Another major strategy for strengthening your vocabulary is analyzing the context in which a particular word appears. In other words, you can often interpret a word's specific meaning by examining its relationship to other words in the sentence. To add power to your speech and writing, you must understand how a word interacts with other words. Not only must you know the meaning of the word but you must be able to determine its function within a sentence. While your ability to cluster root elements, suffixes, and prefixes will help you to recognize words and their functions, it will also help you to manipulate words to create specific parts of speech needed in your sentences.

In reading, writing, or speaking, you must work with a word's specific meaning, its position as a part of speech, and its role as a contributor to the tone or feeling of a sentence. Your sensitivity to a word's tone is a direct result of your vocabulary power. Your command of a word's precise meaning and complex connotations will help you to understand that a word undergoes subtle changes when its context changes. You will also be able to choose between synonyms, fitting the best word into a sentence to capture, create, or emphasize a certain tone. And you will learn to recognize the words that signal meaning and shifts of tone within a sentence. For example, clue words such as *yet, but, although, nevertheless,* and *so on* can help you interpret the correct meaning called for by the context of the sentence. In later parts, we explain many more ways to use your knowledge of grammar and sentence construction to increase your powers of expression.

Part I

THE BUILDING BLOCKS OF WORDS

This book aims to enrich your powers of expression by showing you how to make fine distinctions between words. Unlike other books, this one makes learning the building blocks of words as easy as possible. Most books give you long lists of essentially meaningless and unrelated syllables. Here you'll learn the English concept first, and then a complete grouping of related prefixes, root elements, or suffixes.

For example, words pertaining to speech, such as "talking" or "saying," will be easier for you to remember after you've studied the list *dic, loqu, loc, voc, cit.*

Closely related words or concepts are grouped in the building block study list, so that right after the "speech" building blocks, you will find the "crying out" and "laughing" and "asking" building blocks. By using this approach, you will not only be increasing your recognition of individual words, but also of synonyms and antonyms.

Learning to recognize the building blocks is the essential tool in improving your vocabulary power. The next step is to see how just one building block can branch out and grow into many different words representing different parts of speech, e.g., irritate, irritability, irritant, etc. Here is where your understanding of suffixes will help. Each suffix clearly identifies a word's grammatical function in a sentence. You'll learn, for instance, that all words ending in *-ist* are nouns, and in *-ize* are verbs. So you will be able to recognize both the word's meaning *and* its proper function within a sentence.

Let's look at the building blocks of a fairly common word, *reincarnation*. By splitting the word up into its individual building blocks, you have a prefix *re*, another prefix *in*, a suffix *tion*, and a root element *carn* joined with the vowel *a*. Now, by reassembling these blocks using their English equivalent meaning, you get, roughly, "again-in-the-flesh-act-of" or, more smoothly, "the act of being back in bodily form." Quite a mouthful in just one word!

Clustering on the Building Blocks

The reason for learning to interpret and reassemble the building blocks of a word does not end here. The next step—clustering—is the master key to increasing your vocabulary power. Look at the root element *carn*. How many other words can you think of that have the same root element? Carnival, carnivore, carnal, incarnate, carnage—the list can go on and on.

Historically, a *carnival* was a festive occasion where roasted meats were sold before a period of fasting such as Lent; today the word refers solely to a festive, circus-like event. A *carnivore* is a flesh-eating animal. *Carnal* means having to do with bodily appetites and desires. *Incarnate* means "in the flesh." And *carnage* refers to a terrible massacre, conjuring up visions of a field strewn with bodies. You can see the common denominator around which all of these words cluster.

You've now learned that suffixes signal the grammatical function of words, and that root elements are cores for clustering whole families of words. Prefixes, too, are powerful sources for clustering. As small as they are, they can transform the meaning of a word or root element in much the same way as different prepositions can change the meaning of an entire sentence.

Look what happens to the simple root element *gress* (to step or move forward) when you start switching prefixes: regress, progress, retrogress, transgress, egress, digress. To move again, to move forward, to step back, to move against, to step out, to move in two directions. And when you branch out again by changing suffixes (transgression, retrogressive, etc.), you can see the limitless possibilities for increasing your vocabulary power.

One of the keys to building a powerful vocabulary is learning how to *think visually*. This may sound like a strange piece of advice, but when you realize that each of the common building blocks of the English language has a distinct visual meaning, you'll understand the wisdom of that suggestion. For example, the prefix *pre* means *before*, and the prefix *tele* means far. If you can get into the habit of visualizing the meanings of the different "bits" of a word, you can start to remember its meaning much more quickly. When you encounter the word *preview*, you can think of yourself sitting in a movie theater alone, *watching* a new movie *before* anyone else has had the chance. When you encounter the word *telepathy*, you can picture yourself standing *far* away from someone, yet *feeling* the same thing he or she is feeling, even at that distance.

Your mental image of a word's meaning is the clue to incorporating it into your *functional vocabulary*. A word that was only vaguely familiar to you, part of your *recognition vocabulary*, can suddenly become a word you use and easily remember. By the same token, when you are trying to think of the exact word you need to describe something, you can translate what you're thinking or seeing into a sharp mental image—and reach for the building blocks that express it. For example, imagine yourself talking with a person who is so angry at that moment that his face is *twisted out of shape*. Later, in trying to describe this to someone as quickly, accurately, and economically as possible, you reach for *dis* (poorly, badly) and *tort* (twisted) and find the precise word to describe his face—*distorted*. Here then is the key to unlocking the richness of language—finding the way to express *in one word* the meaning implied in many words.

The many exercises included in this book are designed to help you build and use a power vocabulary. Interspersed throughout the text, they challenge you to increase your functional vocabulary base by applying the concepts presented in the text.

In Challenge 1 on page 8, we've constructed a grid in which you must combine and recombine word elements. To complete the grid, take the given prefix (along the left side of the page) and combine it with the root element specified at the top of the page. Write the new "clustered" word in the matching grid space, working across the page to form a list of new words. We've completed a few grid spaces to get you started.

As mentioned before, most of our higher-level words come from Latin and Greek building blocks. Remember the example of *carnival?* The historical meaning pertained to roasted meat, something not relevant to us today. Obviously, meanings change over the years. Try not to be too rigidly literal when you interpret word meanings from building blocks. Rather, use the building blocks as flexible tools, to unlock a word's current meaning.

Spellings, too, have changed over the years. Knowing something about some of the patterns of change can help you identify the building blocks of even more words. The building blocks can sometimes be disguised. Most of the changes in spelling patterns have occured simply to make words easier to pronounce. For example, you'll often find a vowel joiner (*a,e,i,o,u*) between the root element and a suffix. Such vowels have absolutely no effect on the meaning of a word; they just make it easier to pronounce.

Another spelling pattern to watch for is what happens when a prefix such as *in* (not) is added to words such as *legible, responsible,* or *material.* Instead of their joining to become *inlegible, inresponsible,* or *inmaterial* (all difficult to say), the *n* disappears and the initial consonant of the root element doubles forming the words *illegible, irresponsible,* and *immaterial.* Words or root elements frequently undergo this kind of spelling change when joined to a prefix.

There are many such examples of the dynamic nature of language. You're already accustomed to the irregular spelling of English verb forms (*eat, ate, eaten; swim, swam, swum*). And many words are combinations of pieces of other words or have grown out of foreign terms, as will be seen in Part 2.

Now that you've seen the possibilities for increasing your vocabulary by learning prefixes, suffixes, and root elements, let's take a closer look at them. The following lists illustrate the wide variety of word elements available to us and the almost endless possibilities they offer for increasing your vocabulary power.

Challenge 1: Clustering on the Building Blocks

Root Element

Prefix	SPEC, SPIC	JECT	DUC(T)	MIT, MIS	POS, PON	FER	SCRIP, SCRIB	CLAUS, CLOS, CLUD
AB		ABJECT						
AD			ADDUCE					
CON				COMMIT				
DE					DEPOSE			
E(X)						EFFERENT		
IN							INSCRIBE	
INTER								
INTR( )								
OB								
PER								
PRE								
PRO								
RE								
SUB								
TRANS								

Word Elements: The Building Blocks of English Words

Prepositions	PREFIXES	
Before, toward	fore-	forewarned (warned ahead of time)
	pre-	predisposed (disposed toward)
	ante-	antebellum (before the war)
	pro-	project (throw ahead)
After	post-	postmortem (after death)
With, together	cor-	correlate (show relationship with)
	col-	collaborate (work together)
	con-	contact (in touch with)
	syn-	synchronize (occur at the same time)
	com-	compose (create from parts)
Against	anti-	antipathy (opposing feelings)
	contra-	contradictory (opposite meaning)
	counter-	counterclockwise (in the opposite direction of the clock)
	ob-	obscure (difficult to perceive)
	with-	withstanding (holding up against)
Away, from	ab-	abstain (refrain from)
	apo-	apology (expression of regret)
To, toward	ad-	advancement (moving ahead)
Above, over	hyper-	hypersensitive (extremely sensitive)
	sup(e)r-	supernatural (above and beyond the natural)
Under, below	hypo-	hypoglycemic (having low blood sugar)
	sub-	submarine (below the sea)
	subter-	subterfuge (plot; running beneath the obvious)
	infra-	infrastructure (skeleton; structure beneath the surface)
In, into, within	in-	induct (lead or bring into)
	intr-	intravenous (within the veins)
	endo-	endoderm (within the skin)
	en-	enclosed (contained within)
	em-	embody (incorporate)
Out of, outside	ex-	expel (push out)
	extra-	extraterrestrial (coming from beyond Earth)
	ecto-	ectoderm (top layer of skin)
	e-	elected (chosen from)
Around	circum-	circumlocution (talking around a subject)
	peri-	perimeter (measurement around)

Prepositions

Down, from	de-	decline (slope downward
	cata-	catapult (to hurl from)
Through, across	dia-	diameter (measurement across)
	trans-	transfer (carry to another place)
	per-	percolate (pass or ooze through)
On	epi-	epigraph (inscription on statue or building)
Between	inter-	international (between nations)
Beyond	extra-	extraordinary (beyond the ordinary)
	para-	paramedic (one who works alongside doctors)
	meta-	metamorphosis (changing into another form)
	ultra-	ultrasonic (beyond sound)
Without, not	in-	insecure (not secure)
	an-	anachronism (not in the right time)
	a-	apathy (without emotion)
Far	tele-	telescope (instrument magnifying far objects)
Back, again	re-	recurrent (happening again and again)
Backwards	retro-	retrospect (looking back; hindsight)
Aside	se-	seduce (lead astray)
Behind	poster-	posterior (behind or rearside)

Quantifiers

Many	multi-	multi-faceted (many-sided)
	poly-	polychromatic (many-colored)
All	omni-	omnipotent (all-powerful)
	pan-	panorama (unlimited view)
Both	ambi-	ambiguous (having more than one meaning)
	amphi-	amphibian (creature able to live in two environments)
More	plu-	plural (more than one)
Equal	equi-	equidistant (equally far from two points)
	par-	parity (equality)
Half	semi-	semitransparent (partially see-through)
	hemi-	hemisphere (half of a sphere)
	demi-	demigod (half-man, half-god)
Middle	medi-	median (middle)
	meso-	mesoderm (middle layer of skin)
None	null-	nullify (cancel)
	nihil-	annihilate (destroy)
Enough	sat-	saturated (completely filled)
Whole	holo-	holocaust (destruction by fire)

Quantifiers

First, most	primo-	primogeniture (first-born)
	arch-	archetype (prime example)
	proto-	prototype (original model)
Last	ulti-	ultimatum (last offer or command)
One	uni-	unified (made into one from many)
	mono-	monotonous (one sound or tone)
	sol-	solitary (alone)
Two	du-	duet (twosome)
	di-	dissect (cut into two)
	bi-	biennial (occurring every two years)
Three	tri-	triangle (shape having three angles)
Four	quad-	quadruped (four-footed creature)
	tetra-	tetralogy (series of four plays)
Five	quint-	quintuplets (five children born simultaneously of the same mother)
	penta-	pentagon (shape having five sides)
Six	sex-	sextuplicate (six-fold)
	hexa-	hexagon (shape having six sides)
Seven	sept-	septuagenarian (seventy-year old person)
	hepta-	Heptateuch (first seven books of the Old Testament)
Eight	octo-	octopus (eight-limbed sea creature)
Nine	nov-	novena (prayer lasting nine days)
	non-	nonet (group of nine people)
Ten	dec-	decathalon (ten-skill Olympic event)
Hundred	cent-	century (one hundred years)
	hec(t)-	hectogram (metric unit equalling one hundred grams)
Thousand	mill-	millipede (thousand-footed)
	kilo-	kilogram (one thousand grams)
Not	un-	uncovered (not covered)
	non-	nonessential (not essential)
	a-	apathetic (having no emotion)
	an-	anaerobic (without oxygen)
	in-	insufficient (not sufficient)

SUFFIXES

Modifiers: Adjectives and Adverbs

Like, capable of being	-able	agreeable (capable of agreeing)
	-ible	terrible (like terror)
	-il	civil (capable of being part of society)
	-ile	infantile (like an infant)

Modifiers: Adjectives and Adverbs

Like, pertaining to	-ous	gaseous (pertaining to gas)
	-ine	porcine (piglike)
	-ic	artistic (pertaining to art)
	-ical	political (pertaining to politics)
	-ive	successive (pertaining to a sequence)
	-ac	maniac (pertaining to mania)
Resembling	-some	loathsome (resembling something hateful)
	-like	childlike (like a child)
	-ly	diabolically (like a devil)
	-ish	girlish (like a girl)
	-oid	schizoid (resembling a split)
Belonging to	-ary	military (of the armed forces)
	-ory	sensory (of the senses)
	-an	sylvan (of the forest)
Causing	-fic	horrific (causing horror)
Excessively	-ose	morose (excessively morbid)

Nouns

Act or quality of	-ism	heroism (bravery)
	-ation	hesitation (act of hesitating)
	-ure	torture (act of twisting to hurt)
	-tion	clarification (act of clearing up)
	-ment	contentment (quality of being content)
	-acy	lunacy (act of being a lunatic)
	-itude	magnitude (quality of size)
State or quality of	-ry	rivalry (being rivals)
	-hood	nationhood (being a nation)
	-ship	hardship (difficult times)
	-ness	happiness (being happy)
	-age	marriage (being married)
	-ity	irritability (being irritable)
	-ance	attendance (being present)
	-ence	independence (being independent)
	-ia	hypothermia (having too low temperature)
One who	-er	plumber (one who practices plumbing)
	-ar	liar (one who lies)
	-ary	reactionary (one who dislikes new ideas)
	-or	actor (one who acts)
	-ent	student (one who studies)
	-ant	assistant (one who assists)
	-ist	dentist (one who works with teeth)

Nouns

Result or product of	-ment	entanglement (being tangled up)
	-sis	narcosis (unconsciousness caused by drugs)
Rank or status	-ian	patrician (one of the founding families)

Verbs

To make	-en	enliven (make lively)
	-ate	concentrate (focus on one thing)
	-ize	energize (infuse with energy)
	-fy	terrify (cause terror)

ROOT ELEMENTS

Good, well	well-	wellbeing (health)
	bene-	benefactor (one who does good deeds)
	bon-	bonus (reward for good work)
	eu-	eulogist (one who speaks well of another)
Wrong, bad	mal-	malodorous (having a bad odor)
	dis-	disjointed (crooked)
	dif-	difficult (hard to do)
	mis-	misnomer (inaccurate name)
Same	homo-	homogeneous (uniform throughout)
	simul-	simultaneous (happening at the same time)
Other, another	hetero-	heterodox (having different beliefs)
	ali-	alien (one who is foreign)
	alter-	alternative (another choice)
Large, great	magn-	magnanimous (generous; great-hearted)
	macro-	macrobiosis (longevity)
	maxi-	maximum (the most)
	mega-	megaphone (instrument for enlarging sound)
Small	min-	miniature (small reproduction)
	micro-	microscope (instrument for viewing small objects)
New	neo-	neonatal (newborn)
	nov-	novice (beginner)
Old	ger-	geriatrics (care of the aged)
	paleo-	paleolithic (of the old stone age)
	vet-	veteran (an old soldier)
	sen-	senior (elder)
True	ver-	veracity (truthfulness)
False	pseudo-	pseudonym (false name)

Fast	celer-	accelerate (go faster and faster)
Slow	tard-	tardy (late)
Short	brev-	brevity (shortness; briefness)
High	acro-	acrophobia (fear of heights)
	alti-	altimeter (instrument for measuring altitude)
Heavy	grav-	aggravate (make worse)
Strong	vali-	valiant (brave)
	fort-	fortify (strengthen)
Wise	soph-	philosopher (one who loves wisdom)
	sag-	sagacious (having great wisdom)
Hard	dur-	durable (hardy)
Soft	len-	lenient (permissive)
	moll-	emollient (skin softener)
Pleasing	grat-	ingratitude (not showing pleasure or thanks)
Hidden	crypt-	cryptic (mysterious)
Wide	lat-	latitude (measurement of width)
Straight	rect-	rectitude (moral uprightness)
	ortho-	orthodontist (dentist who straightens teeth)
Sharp	acr-	acrid (bitter)
	acu-	acuity (keenness of wit or senses)
Move	mov-	immovable (not able to be moved)
	mob-	mobile (capable of moving)
	mot-	motility (quality of being able to move)
	kine-	kinetics (pertaining to motion)
Move forward	grad-	graduate (move forward in school)
	gress-	progressive (pertaining to forward motion)
Lean, climb	clin-	inclination (quality of leaning toward)
	cliv-	proclivity (tendency)
	scend-	descend (climb down from)
Tend toward	verg-	converge (come close together)
Cling	her-	adhere (cling or stick to)
	hes-	cohesion (state of sticking together)
Twist	tort-	contortion (act of twisting out of shape)
	tors-	torsion (stress caused by turning)
Turn	ver-	revert (turn back)
	stroph-	catastrophe (terrible turn of events)
	rot-	rotate (turn round and round)
Bend	flec-	deflect (bounce off)
Break	rupt-	disrupt (break up)
	frag-	fragment (break into pieces)
	fract-	fracture (a break or crack)

Fall	cad-	cadence (rhythmic flow)
	cid-	coincidental (happening at the same time by chance)
	cas-	cascade (waterfall)
Roll	volv-	revolver (gun with rotating chamber)
	volut-	revolution (state of turmoil and change)
Hang, weigh	pend-	suspended (hung)
Whirl, spin	turb-	turbulent (constantly moving)
	gyr-	gyrate (whirl)
Flow	flu-	fluent (speaking easily)
	fluv-	effluvial (pertaining to rivers or floods)
Stretch	ten-	tense (strained; nervous)
Bring, carry	fer-	transfer (carry across)
	port-	portable (able to be carried)
Stand	stab-	instability (state of not being stable)
	stat-	stationary (fixed in one place)
Sit, stay, place	pon-	postponed (delayed until a later date)
	posit-	position (placement)
	sed-	sedentary (sitting most of the time)
	sess-	session (meeting)
Lie	cumb-	recumbent (reclining)
Send	mit-	transmit (send across)
	mis-	missile (projectile)
Close	claus-	claustrophobia (fear of closed places)
	clos-	enclosure (closed-in place)
	clud-	exclude (close out)
Clap	plode-	explode (blow out)
Throw	jac-	ejaculation (abrupt ejection)
	jec-	reject (refuse; turn away)
Hold	ten-	tenant (one who lives in another's property)
	tain-	retain (keep)
Hold in	hibit-	inhibit (keep within)
Pour	fus-	confuse (mix up)
Cleanse	purg-	expurgate (remove objectionable material)
Cut	sect-	bisect (cut in two)
Cut, kill	cid-	insecticide (insect killer)
	cis-	incision (cut)
Injure	noc-	innocuous (harmless)
Measure	meter-	thermometer (instrument measuring heat)
	mens-	dimension (shape and measurement)
Manage	nomy-	astronomy (study of the stars)
Mark	stig-	instigate (to spur on)

Owe	deb-	indebtedness (state of being in debt)
Fill	comp-	completion (act of fulfilling)
Empty	vac-	vacant (uninhabited)
Pull	tract-	contraction (a pulling together)
Push, drive	pel-	propel (push forward)
	puls-	repulsion (act of pushing away)
Join	junct-	disjunction (state of being poorly connected)
Separate	cess-	incessant (without stop)
Loosen	solv-	solvent (financially sound)
	solut-	solution (answer to problem)
Bind	string-	stringent (severe)
	strict-	restricted (limited)
Free	lib-	liberate (to set free)
Take	cap-	capture (act of taking by force)
	cep-	accept (taking in)
Give	dat-	mandate (a given order)
	don-	donation (gift)
	dot-	antidote (medicine given to counteract harmful substances)
Go	ced-	precede (go before)
	ces-	procession (formal march)
Come	ven-	advent (arrival)
I	ego-	egocentric (self-centered)
Self	auto-	autograph (personal signature)
	sui-	suicide (self-murder)
Name	nom-	nominate (name someone)
	nym-	pseudonym (false name)
Body, flesh	carn-	carnivore (flesh-eater)
	corp-	corpulent (very fat)
	soma-	psychosomatic (bodily symptoms caused by the mind)
Skin	derm-	dermatitis (skin rash)
	cut-	cuticle (skin at base of fingernails)
Man	anthro-	anthropology (study of mankind)
	homo-	hominid (manlike)
	vir-	virility (manliness)
Woman	gyn-	misogyny (hatred of women)
Child	ped-	pediatrics (child medicine)
Origin, birth	gen-	genesis (beginning; birth)
Born	nat-	native (born in a particular place)
End	fin-	infinite (endless)
	term-	terminate (to end)

Life	viv-	vivacious (lively)
	vit-	vitality (health and energy)
	zoo-	zoology (study of animals)
	bio-	biography (life story)
Breath, life	spir-	respiration (breathing)
Death	mori-	moribund (dying)
	mort-	immortal (never-dying)
	thana-	euthanasia (mercy-killing)
Father	pat(e)r-	patriotism (love of the fatherland)
Mother	mat(e)r-	maternal (motherly)
Brother	frater-	fraternity (brotherhood)
	adelph-	Philadelphia (brotherly love)
Sister	soror-	sorority (sisterhood)
Son	fil-	filial (of a son)
Friend	ami-	amity (friendship)
Circle	orb-	orbit (travel in a circle)
	cycl-	bicycle (two-wheeler)
Ship	nau-	nautical (pertaining to sailing)
Stone	petr-	petrify (turn to stone)
	lith-	lithography (stone-printing)
Carving	glyph-	hieroglyphics (wall paintings of ancient Egypt)
	sculp-	sculptor (carver)
Money	pecun-	impecunious (without money; penniless)
	lucr-	lucrative (producing money; profitable)
Road	via-	viaduct (waterway)
Head	cap-	captain (head officer)
Foot	ped-	centipede (hundred-footed insect)
	pod-	podiatrist (foot doctor)
	pus-	octopus (eight-limbed sea creature)
Hand	manu-	manufacture (make by hand)
	chiro-	chiropractor (doctor who treats disorders with massage)
Sleep	dorm-	dormitory (place for sleeping)
	somn-	insomnia (sleeplessness)
	sopor-	soporific (sleep-inducing)
	hypno-	hypnotic (trancelike)
	morph-	morphine (drug which induces sleepiness)
	com-	coma (unconsciousness)
Wall	mur-	mural (wall painting)
Holy	sacr-	sacrifice (offering to the gods)
	sanct-	sanctimonious (falsely pious)
	hier-	hieroglyphics (sacred carvings)

God	dei-	deification (making into a god)
	theo-	theologian (one who studies religion)
Government by, rule	cracy-	democracy (rule of the people)
Crowd	greg-	congregation (a gathering together)
Rule	dom-	dominate (rule over)
Ruler, leader	arch-	matriarch (female leader)
	gogue-	demagogue (leader who uses mob passions)
People	pleb-	plebian (common)
	demo-	demographics (study of different groups of people)
	pop-	popularity (liked by many people)
Peace	pac-	pacific (peaceful)
War	belli-	bellicose (warlike)
Conquer	vinc-	invincible (unconquerable)
	vict-	victory (winning over opponent)
	vanqu-	vanquish (conquer)
Lead	duc-	induction (initiation)
City	polit-	political (pertaining to politics)
	polis-	metropolis (a chief or capitol city)
	civ-	civilian (non-military person)
Struggle	agon-	antagonistic (one who fights against)
Earth	geo-	geology (study of the earth)
	terr-	territory (land)
Wind	vent-	ventilate (let air in)
Day	diu-	diurnal (daily)
	dia-	diary (written account of daily events)
	jour-	journey (day trip)
Year	ann-	annual (yearly)
Night	noct-	nocturnal (nightly)
Cold	cryo-	cryosurgery (surgery using intense cold to make incisions)
Heat	therm-	geothermal (heat from the earth)
Fire	flam-	flammable (easily burned)
	pyro-	pyrotechnics (fireworks)
	ign-	ignite (set aflame)
Burn	caust-	caustic (burning)
Water	aqua-	aquatic (pertaining to water)
	hydro-	hydroelectric (electricity produced by water power)
Sea	mar-	submarine (below the sea)
Moon	lun-	lunar (pertaining to the moon)
	mon-	month (period of days in a moon's cycle)

Sun	sol-	solar (pertaining to the sun)
	helio-	heliocentric (with the sun at the center)
Light	lum-	illuminate (shed light on)
	luc-	lucid (clear)
	photo-	photography ("light writing")
Ray	radi-	radiate (branch out)
Shadow	umbr-	umbrella (object for shielding sun's rays)
Time	chron-	chronology (sequence)
	tempor-	temporary (for a short time)
Time, age	ev-	medieval (of the Middle Ages)
Star	astr-	astronaut (pilot in spaceship)
	stell-	constellation (arrangement of stars)
World, universe	cosm-	microcosm (tiny world)
Place	loc-	dislocated (out of place)
	top-	Utopia ("no place")
	stead-	homestead (living place)
Power	dynam-	dynamics (power; energy)
Believe	cred-	credible (believable)
Opinion	dox-	orthodox (conventional beliefs)
Consider	puta-	computation (act of figuring out)
Wish	vol-	voluntary (done of one's own wish)
Mind, spirit	psych-	psychosomatic (bodily symptoms caused by the mind)
	noia-	paranoia (mental disturbance; out of touch with reality)
Spirit	anima-	inanimate (not alive)
Think, know, sense	sci-	science (methodical study)
	sens-	sensitivity (awareness)
	sent-	sentient (thinking)
	wit-	unwitting (unknowing)
	gnos-	agnostic (one who does not know if God exists)
Hope	sper-	despair (hopelessness)
Speak, talk, say	dic-	dictation (speaking to have words written down)
	loqu-	loquacious (talkative)
	loc-	elocution (formal speech)
	voc-	evocative (calling to mind; reminding)
	cit-	citation (formal summons)
Laugh	ris-	derisive (mocking)
	rid-	ridicule (taunting; making fun of)

Ask, seek	peti-	petition (request)
	quis-	inquisitive (curious)
	quer-	query (ask)
	rog-	interrogate (question)
Warn, remind	mon-	admonition (warning)
Praise	laud-	laudatory (praiseworthy)
Cry out	clam-	exclamation (crying out)
	plor-	implore (beg)
Deceive	fal-	falsify (make false)
Blame	culp-	culprit (guilty person)
Deny	neg-	negate (make null)
Swear	jur-	perjury (false statement under oath)
Jest	joc-	jocular (good-natured; witty)
Game	lud-	ludicrous (silly; foolish)
Writing	scrip-	transcript (written record of conversation)
	graph-	autograph (one's own signature)
	gram-	telegram (written message transmitted over distance)
	scrib-	scribble (illegible writing)
Learn	cogn-	recognize (remember)
Word	verb-	verbose (wordy)
Read, choose	lect-	lectern (podium, a stand for a speaker)
	leg-	illegible (not readable)
Book	lib-	library (place for books)
	biblio-	bibliography (list of books used in research)
Teach	doc-	indoctrinate (instruct in set of principles or beliefs)
	tut-	tutor (one who teaches)
	tui-	intuition (hunch; mental "voice" that guides)
Study, word	logy-	biology (study of living things)
Remember	mne-	amnesia (state of forgetting)
Forget	obliv-	oblivious (unaware)
Care	cur-	secure (cared for)
Heart	cord-	cordial (from the heart)
	card-	cardiac (pertaining to the heart)
Feelings, suffering	path-	pathetic (pertaining to emotions)
	pass-	passion (intense feelings)
Love	amor-	amorous (pertaining to love)
	phil-	philanthropy (generosity to mankind)
Fear	phobia-	agrophobia (fear of open spaces)
Sin	pecc-	impeccable (having no faults)
Healing	iatr-	psychiatry (healing of the mind)

Faith	fid-	fidelity (faithfulness)
	tru-	trust (faith in another)
See, look	spec-	spectacle (a show)
	vid-	videotape (tape for viewing)
	vis-	visibility (capable of being seen)
	scop-	telescope (instrument magnifying far objects)
	scrut-	scrutinize (examine)
Touch, feel	tang-	tangible (capable of being touched)
	tact-	contact (in touch with)
Feel, sense	(a)esthe-	anaesthesia (state of numbness or unconsciousness)
Hearing, sound	son-	ultrasonic (beyond sound)
	phon-	telephone (instrument carrying sound over distance)
	aud-	inaudible (not able to be heard)
	acou-	acoustics (study of sound)
Silence	tac-	tacit (unspoken)
Eat	vor-	voracious (extremely hungry)
Gnaw	rod-	erode (to wear away)
	ros-	corrosive (chemically dissolve)
Form, shape	morph-	metamorphosis (changing into another form)
Skill, craft	techni-	technique (method of doing something)
Build	struct-	construction (act of building)
Grow	cre-	increments (small stages of growth)
Increase	aug-	augment (add to)
Change	mut-	mutation (change)
Shape	form-	formulation (putting into formal shape)
Use	sum-	consumption (using up)
Make, do	ag-	agent (one who does)
	act-	activate (put into action)
	fac-	manufacture (make by hand)
	fic-	fiction (made-up)
Work	oper-	operate (work on)
	labor-	collaborate (work together)
Walk	ambu-	perambulation (walking around)
	patet-	peripatetic (travelling all over)
Run	curr-	concurrent (happening at the same time)
	curs-	excursion (trip)
Flee	fug-	fugitive (one who flees)
Follow	sequ-	sequential (following)
	sec-	consecutive (following in order)

Wander	err-	erratic (wandering from the ordinary; unreliable)
	migr-	migrant (wanderer)
Jump	sault-	assault (attack)
	sult-	insult (attack verbally)
	sil-	resilience (ability to bounce back)
	sal-	salient (conspicuous)

Clustering on the Parts of Speech

One of the fastest—and most often overlooked—methods of expanding your word power is to increase your knowledge of the many variations of a basic word. Sound confusing? Just think for a minute: English is one of the most flexible languages in the world. We readily take a verb, change it a little and make it become a noun, an adjective, or an adverb. If you remember that suffixes help you to recognize the parts of speech, then you'll immediately see the value of this level of clustering.

Take a look at the example we've provided for Challenge 2 on page 24. We've chosen two common "motion" word elements (*trud* and *gress*) and provided their basic meaning. Next we have clustered on the prefixes that can attach themselves to each of the root elements to change the meaning of the basic word. Then we have clustered on the suffixes that give a word its many different forms.

Reading across the chart, the column heads direct you to:

1. Add a prefix of a particular meaning
2. Provide the verb form made by the specific prefix and root
3. Provide the verbals made by adding *ing* or *ed* to the prefix + root
4. Provide the adjective forms built around the prefix + root by adding the adjective suffixes: *ive, ial,* and *ose*
5. Provide the adverb form of the prefix + root by adding the common adverb suffix *ly*
6. Provide proper noun forms by adding such suffixes as *er, or, ar* or *ist*
7. Provide abstract noun forms by adding such suffixes as *ion, ship, ism* or *hood*

Use the blank chart on page 25 to create your own word clusters built around the root elements *turb, flect,* and *jac, jec.*

Clustering for Synonyms

Probably the most subtle—and difficult—step in building a powerful vocabulary is learning how to choose *exactly* the word you need from among the many choices available to you. As we've mentioned, English is a language rich in clusters of words with similar meanings—synonyms. Yet, as you've also learned, each one of those words has a slightly different meaning, a slightly different shading, a slightly more appropriate context than does the next one. So how do you know which to choose?

There is no one simple solution. As you become more at ease with words, you'll become more adept at choosing the best word. But there are several guidelines you can use to make the overall task much simpler in the long run. The most important

Challenge 2: Clustering on the Parts of Speech—Example

ROOT ELEMENT: *trud*   MEANING: to thrust   CLUSTER: extrude, protrude, intrude

Prefix Meaning	Verb	Verbals	Adjective	Adverb	Concrete Noun	Abstract Noun
out of	extrude	extruding, extruded	extrusive	extrusively	extruder	extrusion
before, forward	protrude	protruding, protruded	protrusive	protrusively		protrusion
in, into	intrude	intruding, intruded	intrusive	intrusively	intruder	intrusion

ROOT ELEMENT: *gress*   MEANING: to move, step   CLUSTER: disgress, egress, regress, retrogress, progress, congress, transgress

Prefix Meaning	Verb	Verbals	Adjective	Adverb	Concrete Noun	Abstract Noun
two	digress	digressing, digressed	digressive	digressively	digresser	digression
out of					egress	egression
again	regress	regressing, regressed	regressive	regressively		regression
backward	retrogress	retrogressing, retrogressed	retrogressive	retrogressively		retrogression
forward	progress	progressing, progressed	progressive	progressively	progress, progressive	progression
with	congress	congressing, congressed	congressional		congress, congressionalist	
across	transgress	transgressing, transgressed	transgressive		transgressor	transgression

Challenge 2: Clustering on the Parts of Speech—Exercise

ROOT ELEMENT: *turb* MEANING: _____ CLUSTER: _____

Prefix Meaning	Verb	Verbals	Adjective	Adverb	Concrete Noun	Abstract Noun

ROOT ELEMENT: *flect* MEANING: _____ CLUSTER: _____

Prefix Meaning	Verb	Verbals	Adjective	Adverb	Concrete Noun	Abstract Noun

ROOT ELEMENT: *jac, jec* MEANING: _____ CLUSTER: _____

Prefix Meaning	Verb	Verbals	Adjective	Adverb	Concrete Noun	Abstract Noun

guideline to remember is the importance of thinking visually—of learning the physical, visual meaning of each of the building blocks of the english language.

An example will help you see the point. Take a relatively simple word such as *shake*. If you were to list words at random that closely matched that meaning, you might come up with the following list: shimmy, flutter, wobble, quiver. Look at them again—they all share the basic meaning of the motion involved. Yet if they all meant exactly the same thing as *shake* we wouldn't need any of them. So how do we know when one is more accurate to use than another? Think visually! What shimmies? How, exactly, would you describe what shimmying is? Aha! You think of the tires on your car when they aren't balanced properly; you sense that rapid vibration, the tiny sensation of a "little" shake. Now think of flutter—what flutters? Eyelashes . . . bird's wings . . . leaves falling to the ground. Again, the idea of shaking is there, but this time with a distinct difference—things that flutter do so horizontally! Let's try wobble. Yes, it's a kind of shaking . . . but it's irregular, unsteady. Visualize what someone looks like—their knees, especially—when they've had a bad fright. Think of a precariously balanced vase on the edge of a rickety table. That's wobble! Now for quiver. A child trying not to cry—think of his lips! A frightened puppy cowering under the chair—think of how it "shakes." That tiny, rapid "shake" is a *quiver.*

And you thought *shake* was an easy concept! But the point is clear—whether you're dealing with technical vocabularies or everyday conversation, real word power lies in being able to choose *exactly* the right word. A strong command of the prefix, suffix, and root element lists will help you develop this word power. As mentioned, we grouped the word elements together so that you could more easily recognize related words when you encountered them.

Another point: there's no real rule for whether the best word you choose is *right* or *wrong*. The only measure should be whether it does the job of communicating your ideas accurately and appropriately. Part of this involves being sensitive to the reader and listener—should you be using formal, technical language or informal, conversational language? Clear, effective communication is the ultimate goal of vocabulary power, so always keep your reader's or listener's needs in mind.

The next challenge should help you become more aware of the subtle shades of meaning from which you have to choose. It's the only exercise in the book for which there is no answer key, because only you can decide how best to categorize these sample words. If any of them are unfamiliar to you, then by all means check your word list or *Webster's New World Dictionary*. Just remember to think visually and to make every word you choose express both your intended meaning and your intended *intensity* of meaning.

Challenge 3: Synonyms

Below is a random list of words that are roughly synonymous with the word *glad*. On a scale of one to five, assign each word a level of intensity, with five being the most intense, one being neutral, mild, or roughly equivalent with the intensity of glad.

happy	rapturous	pleased	gratified
blissful	exultant	elated	spirited
ecstatic	transported	joyful	lighthearted
exuberant	rhapsodic	gleeful	merry
jolly	jubilant	contented	optimistic
mirthful	cheerful	rejoiced	exhilarated

same	strong	stronger	intense	extreme
(1)	(2)	(3)	(4)	(5)

Now do the same with this list of words roughly synonymous with *sad*.

unhappy	miserable	downcast	troubled
melancholic	disappointed	disconsolate	despairing
sorrowful	discontented	blue	grim
depressed	despondent	brokenhearted	woeful
displeased	pessimistic	lachrymose	mournful
dejected	griefstricken	sorry	distressed

same	strong	stronger	intense	extreme
(1)	(2)	(3)	(4)	(5)

Challenge 4: Hidden Word Elements

Sometimes the word elements we're looking for are hidden due to a process called *assimilation*. Certain consonants, when placed together, are difficult to pronounce, and so, over the years, we've gotten lazy and followed the easiest "route" of pronunciation. When searching for word elements, a good clue to look for is a doubled consonant near the beginning of the word, or where a prefix would most likely be joined to a root element. Each of the following words have hidden word elements, which you should be able to locate and identify as the prefix and root element.

		Prefix		Root
1.	allusion	_____	+	_____
2.	suffuse	_____	+	_____
3.	occlusion	_____	+	_____
4.	irruption	_____	+	_____
5.	corrosive	_____	+	_____
6.	effusive	_____	+	_____
7.	assimilate	_____	+	_____
8.	colloquial	_____	+	_____
9.	succumb	_____	+	_____
10.	offer	_____	+	_____

Challenges 5–8: Building Block Words

In each of the following challenges, the words in the left-hand column are built on word elements given in the previous pages. Match each numbered word with its lettered definition from the right-hand column.

Challenge 5

1.	mutable	a.	able to be touched
2.	culpable	b.	laughable
3.	interminable	c.	of the first age
4.	amiable	d.	holding firmly
5.	vital	e.	necessary to life
6.	primeval	f.	unending
7.	tenacious	g.	unable to be lossened
8.	tangible	h.	changeable
9.	risible	i.	friendly
10.	indissoluble	j.	blameworthy

Challenge 6

1.	infinity	a.	sum paid yearly
2.	duplicity	b.	a throwing out or from
3.	levity	c.	shortness
4.	brevity	d.	endlessness
5.	ejection	e.	killing of a race
6.	edict	f.	lightness of spirit
7.	infraction	g.	a breaking
8.	genocide	h.	doubledealing
9.	annuity	i.	official decree
10.	microcosm	j.	miniature world

Challenge 7

1.	recede	a.	state as the truth
2.	abdicate	b.	throw light on
3.	homogenize	c.	give up a power
4.	illuminate	d.	put into words
5.	supervise	e.	go away
6.	verbalize	f.	oversee
7.	legislate	g.	make laws
8.	intervene	h.	draw out
9.	aver	i.	make the same throughout
10.	protract	j.	come between

Challenge 8

1.	abduction	a.	a coming to
2.	fortitude	b.	a flowing together
3.	consequence	c.	something added to
4.	confluence	d.	coming back to life
5.	status	e.	truthfulness
6.	disunity	f.	result
7.	veracity	g.	strength
8.	revival	h.	lack of oneness
9.	advent	i.	a leading away
10.	adjunct	j.	standing

Challenge 9: Dissecting Words

For each of the following words, write its "parts" in the appropriate column and identify the part of speech its suffix indicates.

Example: reclusive   re   clus   ive   adjective

Word	Prefix	Root(s)	Suffix	Part of Speech
1. peripatetic	_____ +	_____ +	_____	_____
2. impeccable	_____ +	_____ +	_____	_____
3. exculpate	_____ +	_____ +	_____	_____
4. invincible	_____ +	_____ +	_____	_____
5. antagonist	_____ +	_____ +	_____	_____
6. heliocentric	_____ +	_____ +	_____	_____
7. celerity	_____ +	_____ +	_____	_____
8. misanthropic	_____ +	_____ +	_____	_____
9. proclivity	_____ +	_____ +	_____	_____
10. bellicose	_____ +	_____ +	_____	_____

Now that you've identified the building blocks of those words, can you give their meanings?

1. peripatetic   _____
2. impeccable   _____
3. exculpate   _____
4. invincible   _____
5. antagonist   _____
6. heliocentric   _____
7. celerity   _____
8. misanthropic   _____
9. proclivity   _____
10. bellicose   _____

Challenge 10: Prefixes

Each of the following words contains a common English prefix. Underline the prefix, give its basic meaning, and supply another common English word containing the same prefix.

Word	Prefix Meaning	New Word
1. foretell		
2. premonition		
3. antebellum		
4. prorate		
5. postpone		
6. convocation		
7. sympathy		
8. antipathy		
9. obstruct		
10. contradict		
11. countermand		
12. withhold		
13. absolve		
14. apology		
15. advent		
16. hyperkinetic		
17. supersonic		
18. hypodermic		
19. submarine		
20. subterfuge		
21. surname		
22. infrared		
23. inhibit		
24. intramural		
25. endomorphic		

Challenge 11: Root Elements

Each of the following words contains a common English root element. Underline the root element, give its basic meaning, and supply another common English word containing the same root.

Word	Root Element Meaning	New Word
1. premonition		
2. antebellum		
3. postpone		
4. convocation		
5. sympathy		
6. obstruct		
7. contradict		
8. absolve		
9. apology		
10. advent		
11. hyperkinetic		
12. supersonic		
13. hypodermic		
14. submarine		
15. subterfuge		
16. inhibit		
17. intramural		
18. endomorphic		
19. endemic		
20. extraterrestrial		

Challenges 12–15: Word Elements and Suffixes

In each of the following exercises, choose the word element or suffix in the right-hand column that matches the meaning of the word element in the left-hand column.

Challenge 12

1.	ultra	a.	per
2.	counter	b.	with
3.	multi	c.	bi
4.	circum	d.	kilo
5.	du	e.	ob
6.	syn	f.	arch
7.	mill	g.	poly
8.	dia	h.	extra
9.	contra	i.	con
10.	proto	j.	peri

Challenge 14

1.	-able	a.	-ness
2.	-ous	b.	-sis
3.	-tion	c.	-ical
4.	-like	d.	-an
5.	-some	e.	-ist
6.	-ant	f.	-ile
7.	-ary	g.	-oid
8.	-hood	h.	-ment
9.	-ism	i.	-ish
10.	-ment	j.	-itude

Challenge 13

1.	trans	a.	tetra
2.	in	b.	pre
3.	un	c.	sol
4.	equi	d.	super
5.	ante	e.	dia
6.	de	f.	meta
7.	quad	g.	endo
8.	hyper	h.	non
9.	para	i.	par
10.	mono	j.	cata

Challenge 15

1.	bene	a.	scend
2.	macro	b.	gyr
3.	mob	c.	simul
4.	clin	d.	alti
5.	neo	e.	kine
6.	rect	f.	en
7.	stroph	g.	ortho
8.	homo	h.	mega
9.	acro	i.	rot
10.	turb	j.	nov

Challenges 16–19: Identifying Opposites

Choose the word element in the right-hand column that is opposite in meaning from the word element in the left-hand column.

Challenge 16

1.	syn	a.	holo
2.	pre	b.	extra
3.	hemi	c.	anti
4.	hyper	d.	ad
5.	con	e.	null
6.	en	f.	ob
7.	primo	g.	post
8.	omni	h.	super
9.	ab	i.	ulti
10.	infra	j.	sub

Challenge 18

1.	ced	a.	vac
2.	mort	b.	sess
3.	mater	c.	pel
4.	cap	d.	cess
5.	gyn	e.	string
6.	stat	f.	don
7.	comp	g.	nat
8.	junct	h.	ven
9.	solv	i.	pater
10.	tract	j.	anthro

Challenge 17

1.	bon	a.	celer
2.	neo	b.	alter
3.	nov	c.	min
4.	dur	d.	acro
5.	ver	e.	hetero
6.	simul	f.	sen
7.	tard	g.	mal
8.	macro	h.	paleo
9.	homo	i.	moll
10.	brev	j.	pseudo

Challenge 19

1.	lun	a.	therm
2.	laud	b.	clam
3.	ambu	c.	belli
4.	dia	d.	obliv
5.	rid	e.	tac
6.	cryo	f.	culp
7.	tut	g.	helio
8.	mne	h.	curs
9.	pac	i.	noct
10.	son	j.	cogn

Challenge 20: Building Vocabulary Power

Real vocabulary power means being able to express yourself accurately—and economically. See if you can find the one word, created from word elements, which can replace each of these phrases.

1. murder of a king

1. _____

2. to make by hand

2. _____

3. a warning against

3. _____

4. pushing back

4. _____

5. to drag forward

5. _____

6. correct opinion

6. _____

7. light writing

7. _____

8. book lover

8. _____

9. secret writing

9. _____

10. fireworks

10. _____

11. having to do with body and mind

11. _____

12. one who struggles against

12. _____

13. speech given before

13. _____

14. state of not remembering

14. _____

15. without form or shape

15. _____

Challenges 21–22: Can You Match This?

In the following exercises, find the one word in the right-hand column that contains the word element referred to in the left-hand column.

Challenge 21

1.	struggle	a.	cosmopolitan
2.	friend	b.	abbreviate
3.	war	c.	accelerate
4.	short	d.	cryptic
5.	head	e.	protagonist
6.	fast	f.	credential
7.	to fill	g.	capitulate
8.	world	h.	amicable
9.	to believe	i.	rebellion
10.	hidden	j.	comply

Challenge 22

1.	to blame	a.	endure
2.	to lie down	b.	exculpate
3.	to care	c.	conduct
4.	to owe	d.	dominion
5.	ten	e.	succumb
6.	rule	f.	debenture
7.	opinion	g.	dynasty
8.	to lead	h.	curator
9.	hard	i.	paradox
10.	power	j.	decimal

Challenges 23–24: The Building Blocks of English

The words listed on the left are constructed from the common building blocks of the English language. Can you match them up with the words in the right-hand column to find their common definition?

Challenge 23

1.	centennial	a.	before the war
2.	prospective	b.	going against
3.	circumspect	c.	in name only
4.	multinational	d.	hard, unyielding
5.	clamorous	e.	looking forward
6.	antebellum	f.	careful, looking in all directions
7.	contrary	g.	hundred-year anniversary
8.	impassioned	h.	in many countries
9.	obdurate	i.	full of strong feelings
10.	nominal	j.	shouting

Challenge 24

1.	dislocation	a.	wrong name
2.	misanthropy	b.	withdrawal
3.	misnomer	c.	knowing in advance
4.	negation	d.	denial
5.	propulsion	e.	power of will
6.	volition	f.	forerunner
7.	retraction	g.	putting out of place
8.	inclination	h.	pushing forward
9.	precognition	i.	hatred of mankind
10.	precursor	j.	leaning toward

Challenges 25–28: Can You Match This?

Find the word in the right-hand column that contains the root element referred to in the left-hand column.

Challenge 25

1.	on	a.	ingratitude
2.	to deceive	b.	epitaph
3.	son	c.	fraternize
4.	to bend	d.	gravitate
5.	to shape	e.	refuge
6.	brother	f.	deflect
7.	to flee	g.	infallible
8.	origin, birth	h.	generate
9.	pleasing	i.	conformity
10.	heavy	j.	affiliate

Challenge 27

1.	money	a.	permutation
2.	game	b.	mariner
3.	sea	c.	amnesty
4.	mother	d.	abnegation
5.	middle	e.	ludicrous
6.	to remember	f.	mediator
7.	death	g.	astronaut
8.	to change	h.	lucrative
9.	ship	i.	immortal
10.	to deny	j.	matrimony

Challenge 26

1.	crowd	a.	jury
2.	woman	b.	hologram
3.	sun	c.	segregate
4.	half	d.	dilate
5.	whole	e.	jocular
6.	to jest	f.	hemisphere
7.	to join	g.	plausible
8.	to swear	h.	conjunction
9.	to praise	i.	gynecology
10.	wide	j.	helium

Challenge 28

1.	none, nothing	a.	nominee
2.	night	b.	annihilate
3.	name	c.	oblivious
4.	to manage	d.	impending
5.	to forget	e.	repatriate
6.	peace	f.	impecunious
7.	father	g.	nocturnal
8.	sin	h.	impeccable
9.	money	i.	pacify
10.	to hang, weigh	j.	autonomy

Challenges 29–34: Recognizing Word Elements

In each of the following challenges, circle the best answer for each question.

Challenge 29

1. Which of the following words does *not* contain a word element meaning "high"?
   a. acrimonious
   b. acropolis
   c. alto
   d. altimeter

2. Which of the following words does *not* contain a word element meaning "to hear"?
   a. acoustical
   b. auditory
   c. sonagraphy
   d. inaugurate

3. Which of the following words does *not* contain a word element meaning "sharp"?
   a. acumen
   b. exacerbate
   c. acerbic
   d. accumulate

4. Which of the following words does *not* contain a word element meaning "other, another"?
   a. alternate
   b. alien
   c. altimeter
   d. heterodox

5. Which of the following words does *not* contain a word element meaning "to make, do"?
   a. reactionary
   b. manufacture
   c. agitate
   d. terrible

6. Which of the following words does *not* contain a word element meaning "act or quality of"?
   a. demonstration
   b. tenure
   c. fortitude
   d. dentist

7. Which of the following words does *not* contain a word element meaning "like, pertaining to"?
   a. bovine
   b. movable
   c. manic
   d. insomniac

8. Which of the following words does *not* contain a word element meaning "without, not"?
   a. defector
   b. insufficient
   c. amoral
   d. nonsense

9. Which of the following words does *not* contain a word element meaning "away, from"?
   a. absent
   b. apprehend
   c. apology
   d. abrasion

10. Which of the following words does *not* contain a word element meaning "to, toward"?
    a. assimilate
    b. adjunct
    c. adhere
    d. abject

Challenge 30

1. Which of the following words does *not* contain a word element meaning "walk"?
   a. pathetic
   b. amble
   c. ambulatory
   d. peripatetic

2. Which of the following words does *not* contain a word element meaning "love"?
   a. amorphous
   b. amorous
   c. bibliophile
   d. enamored

3. Which of the following words does *not* contain a word element meaning "both"?
   a. amphora
   b. anapest
   c. amphitheatre
   d. ambidextrous

4. Which of the following words does *not* contain a word element meaning "state or quality of"?
   a. brotherhood
   b. radiance
   c. friendship
   d. defendant

5. Which of the following words does *not* contain a word element meaning "spirit, mind"?
   a. paranoia
   b. animation
   c. metamorphosis
   d. psychiatric

6. Which of the following words does *not* contain a word element meaning "year"?
   a. annihilate
   b. biennial
   c. anniversary
   d. annual

7. Which of the following words does *not* contain a word element meaning "man"?
   a. virile
   b. anthropology
   c. arthropod
   d. homonid

8. Which of the following words does *not* contain a word element meaning "against"?
   a. contrary
   b. antedate
   c. antidote
   d. obstruct

9. Which of the following words does *not* contain a word element meaning "before, toward?"
   a. antecedent
   b. foreshadow
   c. former
   d. propel

10. Which of the following words does *not* contain a word element meaning "one who"?
    a. participant
    b. husband
    c. scholar
    d. resident

Challenge 31

1. Which of the following words does *not* contain a word element meaning "to cry out"?
   a. deplore
   b. implosion
   c. exclamation
   d. claimant

2. Which of the following words does *not* contain a word element meaning "to close"?
   a. recluse
   b. preclude
   c. acclimate
   d. enclose

3. Which of the following words does *not* contain a word element meaning "to lean, climb"?
   a. apprehend
   b. proclivity
   c. recline
   d. descend

4. Which of the following words does *not* contain a word element meaning "to learn, know"?
   a. cognizant
   b. sentient
   c. semblance
   d. diagnosis

5. Which of the following words does *not* contain a word element meaning "with, together"?
   a. conference
   b. accommodate
   c. commission
   d. synthetic

6. Which of the following words does *not* contain a word element meaning "to sleep"?
   a. ambulatory
   b. coma
   c. dormant
   d. insomniac

7. Which of the following words does *not* contain a word element meaning "to run"?
   a. recurrent
   b. recumbent
   c. precursor
   d. cursory

8. Which of the following words does *not* contain a word element meaning "circle"?
   a. systematic
   b. orbit
   c. cyclone
   d. recycle

9. Which of the following words does *not* contain a word element meaning "to give"?
   a. data
   b. donor
   c. antedate
   d. antidote

10. Which of the following words does *not* contain a word element meaning "God"?
    a. deity
    b. thanataphobia
    c. theocracy
    d. divinity

Challenge 32

1. Which of the following words does *not* contain a word element meaning "day"?
   a. journalist
   b. diurnal
   c. diarist
   d. diploid

2. Which of the following words does *not* contain a word element meaning "through, across"?
   a. demogogue
   b. dialogue
   c. perambulate
   d. transcontinental

3. Which of the following words does *not* contain a word element meaning "to speak, talk, say"?
   a. vacation
   b. malediction
   c. soliloquy
   d. vocational

4. Which of the following words does *not* contain a word element meaning "wrong, bad"?
   a. misrepresent
   b. malevolent
   c. disabled
   d. massive

5. Which of the following words does *not* contain a word element meaning "to teach"?
   a. doctrine
   b. decency
   c. intuition
   d. tutorial

6. Which of the following words does *not* contain a word element meaning "out of, outside"?
   a. eject
   b. ectopic
   c. extrasensory
   d. educate

7. Which of the following words does *not* contain a word element meaning "in, into, within"?
   a. embrace
   b. enunciate
   c. intravenous
   d. endomorph

8. Which of the following words does *not* contain a word element meaning "equal"?
   a. equanimity
   b. equivocate
   c. parity
   d. appearance

9. Which of the following words does *not* contain a word element meaning "to wander"?
   a. emigrate
   b. erroneous
   c. culpable
   d. aberrant

10. Which of the following words does *not* contain a word element meaning "beyond"?
    a. ectoplasmic
    b. paranoia
    c. metamorphosis
    d. ultrasonic

Challenge 33

1. Which of the following words does *not* contain a word element meaning "to bring, carry"?
   a. fertile
   b. febrile
   c. transport
   d. conference

2. Which of the following words does *not* contain a word element meaning "faith"?
   a. betrothed
   b. fiduciary
   c. truncated
   d. infidel

3. Which of the following words does *not* contain a word element meaning "end"?
   a. defame
   b. terminate
   c. define
   d. determine

4. Which of the following words does *not* contain a word element meaning "fire"?
   a. inflammable
   b. incorrigible
   c. pyretic
   d. igneous

5. Which of the following words does *not* contain a word element meaning "to flow"?
   a. flux
   b. superfluous
   c. influenza
   d. perfidy

6. Which of the following words does *not* contain a word element meaning "strong"?
   a. comfort
   b. farcical
   c. valiant
   d. forceful

7. Which of the following words does *not* contain a word element meaning "to break"?
   a. refraction
   b. rupture
   c. frugal
   d. fragmentary

8. Which of the following words does *not* contain a word element meaning "earth"?
   a. geometry
   b. terrace
   c. terrain
   d. torrid

9. Which of the following words does *not* contain a word element meaning "old"?
   a. invertebrate
   b. senator
   c. gerontology
   d. inveterate

10. Which of the following words does *not* contain a word element meaning "to know, learn"?
    a. unwitting
    b. schematic
    c. nonsensical
    d. science

Challenge 34

1. Which of the following words does *not* contain a word element meaning "small"?
   a. microbe
   b. diminutive
   c. minuscule
   d. dimension

2. Which of the following words does *not* contain a word element meaning "to send"?
   a. remit
   b. missionary
   c. admit
   d. minority

3. Which of the following words does *not* contain a word element meaning "one"?
   a. monologue
   b. uncertainty
   c. disunified
   d. solitary

4. Which of the following words does *not* contain a word element meaning "many"?
   a. polychromatic
   b. multitude
   c. policy
   d. multiply

5. Which of the following words does *not* contain a word element meaning "new"?
   a. noxious
   b. neonatal
   c. neologism
   d. novice

6. Which of the following words does *not* contain a word element meaning "to injure"?
   a. obnoxious
   b. nocturnal
   c. innocuous
   d. innocent

7. Which of the following words does *not* contain a word element meaning "straight"?
   a. correction
   b. rectitude
   c. orthodontist
   d. incurable

8. Which of the following words does *not* contain a word element meaning "all"?
   a. panoramic
   b. polysyllabic
   c. pandemonium
   d. omnivorous

9. Which of the following words does *not* contain a word element meaning "feelings, suffering"?
   a. apathetic
   b. peripatetic
   c. passivity
   d. compassion

10. Which of the following words does *not* contain a word element meaning "foot"?
    a. impassable
    b. impediment
    c. octopus
    d. arthropod

Part II

THE SPECIAL CATEGORIES OF WORDS

Evolved and Invented Words

There are many other ways in which words are formed besides the building block method. Evolved and invented words are perfect examples. *Evolved words* are those which have changed over time—in pronunciation, in spelling, in meaning. *Invented words* are those intentionally formed by either combining more than one word or by combining the first letters in a series of words (an acronym). Each of the following challenges contains lists of common English words that fit into the categories of evolved and invented words, including a list of the names of the days and months, a list of vocabulary derived from myths, and a list of words based on human names. To get started, test your familiarity with the evolved and invented vocabulary in the following challenge.

Challenge 35: Evolved and Invented Words

Match these common evolved and invented words with their meanings.

1.	tawdry	a.	fourteen nights
2.	maudlin	b.	chuckle + snort
3.	scuba	c.	recruit
4.	chortle	d.	housewife
5.	nickname	e.	cheaply made (St. Audrey's laces)
6.	rookie	f.	self-contained underwater breathing apparatus
7.	atone	g.	weepy, sentimental (Mary Magdalene)
8.	smog	h.	to be at one with God
9.	fortnight	i.	an eke name (an "also" name)
10.	hussy	j.	smoke + fog

What's in a Name?

Nothing exemplifies the English language's colorful history better than the words we use for the names of the days of the week and the months, as illustrated in the following challenge.

Challenge 36: What's in a Name?

See if you can match up the following names of the days and months with their origins.

1. Sunday   a. named after Augustus Caesar

2. Monday   b. tenth month

3. Tuesday   c. named after Saturn, ancient Roman god

4. Wednesday   d. named after the Germanic dawn goddess

5. Thursday   e. named after Juno, wife of Jupiter

6. Friday   f. named after Tiw, Germanic god of war and sky

7. Saturday   g. named after Aphrodite, Greek goddess of love

8. January   h. seventh month

9. February   i. named after Janus, two-faced Roman god of beginnings

10. March   j. named after Thor, Germanic god of thunder

11. April   k. the Sun's day

12. May   l. named after Julius Caesar

13. June   m. ninth month

14. July   n. the moon's day

15. August   o. named after Freija, Germanic goddess of love

16. September   p. named after Mars, Roman god of war

17. October   q. named after Maia, Roman goddess of life and beauty

18. November   r. named after Woden, chief Germanic god

19. December   s. named after feast of burning and purification

20. Easter   t. eighth month

Of Myths . . .

One of the most colorful sources of words and phrases in the English language is the classical myths of ancient Greece, Rome, and the Germanic tribes. Although the myths may have faded in the mists of time, the words they inspired are still strong and vibrant today. Here's a collection to increase your own word power.

adonis   a vain and beautiful man

bacchanal   a wild, uninhibited orgy

cassandra   a prophet doomed to be ignored

cornucopia   an abundance; plenty

erotic   pertaining to sexual love

halcyon   peaceful, prosperous times

herculean   requiring tremendous effort

hermetic   secret; sealed

hydra   a complicated problem that must be solved from many different perspectives

iridescent   rainbow-like; colorful

jovial   jolly, hearty

junoesque   a stately, imposing beauty

mercurial   changeable; swift

narcissistic   self-absorbed; exceedingly vain

nemesis   a deadly adversary

odyssey   a long, wandering adventure; a search

olympian   majestic

panic   wild, frightful chaos

phoenix   something that is reborn from its own destruction

promethean   boldly creative; inspirational; life-giving

protean   variable; versatile; creative

saturnine   gloomy; taciturn

stentorian   a loud, deep voice

tantalize   to torment with unattainable things

titanic   powerful; huge

. . . And Men

Myths aren't the only source of unusual words. People real and fictional, famous and infamous, have lent their names to words in use today.

bloomers   loose gathered pants for women; named after the 19th century American feminist Amelia Bloomer

bowdlerize   to edit prudishly; named after Thomas Bowdler, the 18th century Englishman who tried to expurgate the works of Shakespeare

boycott   to abstain in protest as a form of coercion; named after a 19th century Irish land agent who had refused to lower rents

chauvinism   militant and fanatical loyalty; named after Nicholas Chauvin, a devoted follower of Napoleon

draconian   severe, harsh measures; named after Draco, a particularly harsh Athenian lawgiver

galvanize   to stimulate with electricity; to startle into action; named after Luigi Galvani, an Italian scientist

gerrymander   to alter to one's advantage; named after Elbridge Gerry, a 19th century Massachusetts politician who tried to change voting districts to his own advantage

lilliputian   of small intelligence, tiny; named after the tiny people in Jonathan Swift's *Gulliver's Travels*

lothario   a seducer; named after a character in the play *The Fair Penitant* by Nicholas Rowe

lynch   to execute or hang without trial; named after Charles Lynch, an 18th century Justice of the Peace in Virginia

machiavellian   politically expedient, regardless of people's needs or rights; named after Niccolo Machiavelli, author of the Renaissance classic, *The Prince*

martinet   a rigid, militaristic disciplinarian; named after Jean Martinet, a 19th century French general

maverick   a non-conformist; named after Samuel Maverick, a 19th century Texas rancher who refused to brand his cattle

mesmerize   to hypnotize; named after Franz Mesmer, the 18th century Austrian doctor who developed the technique

pander   to pimp, to appeal to someone's lowest instincts; named after Pandarus, the go-between in Chaucer's *Troilus and Criseyde*

philippic   a virulent condemnation; named after a series of speeches given by the Greek philosopher Demosthenes against Philip of Macedon

pyrrhic a victory won with staggering losses; named after the site of a bloody battle between the Epireans and Romans

quixotic blindly idealistic and romantic; named after Cervantes's famous *Don Quixote de la Mancha*

sadism delight in cruelty; named after the perverse French nobleman, the Marquis de Sade

vandal someone who willfully destroys property; named after the Vandals, a Germanic tribe that ravaged Europe during the Dark Ages

Challenge 37: Of Myths and Men

See if you can join the company of the great gods of the ancient world and the giants of the modern by correctly matching the following terms and their definitions.

1. majestic	a. chauvinism
2. powerful	b. draconian
3. prophet doomed to be ignored	c. hermetic
4. exceedingly vain	d. pyrrhic
5. creative	e. promethean
6. to torment	f. olympian
7. deadly adversary	g. machiavellian
8. secret; sealed	h. maverick
9. a search	i. cassandra
10. gloomy	j. narcissistic
11. harsh condemnation	k. tantalize
12. to edit prudishly	l. titanic
13. fanatical loyalty	m. martinet
14. politically expedient	n. galvanize
15. non-conformist	o. odyssey
16. severe harsh measures	p. saturnine
17. rigid disciplinarian	q. nemesis
18. to startle into action	r. bowdlerize
19. won at a great price	s. quixotic
20. idealistic and romantic	t. philippic

Borrowed and Foreign Words

As mentioned earlier, the English language is rich with words from other times and places. And just as there's a history to each word, there's history *in* each word.

Every word we've "borrowed" from another langauge tells a story about the location where an English-speaking person was at the time the word entered the language. The great seafarers, explorers, merchants, and military travelers brought home more than furs, silk, and glories: they brought back the colorful words they had heard and used along the way!

Many of the words that have been borrowed from other languages are actually the specialized vocabularies of certain occupations or creative fields. The French language contributed many words we use today in cooking and fashion, as did Italian in music, Arabic in science and mathematics, and Dutch in shipping.

You may be surprised to discover the origin of many familiar English words in the following lists.

African

boogie-woogie	hep-cat	voodoo	okra
jazz	goober	gumbo	zombie
tango			

Hindi (Indian)

juggernaut	punch	chintz	pajama
pundit	guru	madras	bungalow
shampoo	thug	cheetah	
dungaree	loot	jungle	

Dutch

buoy	freight	bumpkin	schooner
waffle	brandy	boss	scour
landscape	coleslaw	cookie	

Amerindian

caribou	squash	moose	Mississippi
mocassin	wigwam	pecan	hickory
opossum	raccoon	squaw	toboggan
Chicago	succotash	skunk	

Spanish

aficianado	mosquito	cannibal	siesta
bravado	barrio	tornado	cigar
hacienda	desperado	bonanza	vanilla
tobacco	potato	flotilla	
machismo	hurricane	cargo	
junta	renegade	lariat	

Persian

azure	jackal	shawl	rook
emerald	chess	paradise	taffeta
orange	lilac	check	scimitar
sash	pawn	musk	

Arabic

alchemy	bazaar	nadir	mummy
amber	crimson	zero	saffron
chemistry	lute	hazard	talisman
jar	tambourine	giraffe	cipher
naphtha	alcohol	caravan	scirocco
sugar	camphor	damask	admiral
algebra	elixir	mattress	magazine
monsoon	lime	tariff	artichoke
zenith	opium	alkali	cotton
arsenal	syrup	carat	divan
gazelle	almanac	assassin	ottoman

Challenge 38: Borrowed and Foreign Words

Words have entered the English language from all around the world. Check the etymological entry for each word in your dictionary and then match each word with its origins.

1.	tycoon	a.	Polynesian
2.	ketchup	b.	Dutch
3.	taboo	c.	Hindi
4.	alcohol	d.	Amerindian
5.	woodchuck	e.	Italian
6.	whiskey	f.	Welsh
7.	boondocks	g.	Portuguese
8.	umbrella	h.	Hebrew
9.	freight	i.	Hungarian
10.	penguin	j.	Philipino
11.	cinnamon	k.	Gaelic
12.	coach	l.	Arabic
13.	veranda	m.	Japanese
14.	seersucker	n.	Chinese

Latin Terms to Remember

Lawyers and doctors aren't the only people who use Latin phrases and words frequently. Most successful people are familiar with the following Latin expressions. Note that they are italicized; unlike many of the French words we use in English, these are still treated as "foreign" terms.

ad hoc   for a specific, limited purpose

ad nauseam   to a ridiculous or disgusting degree

caveat emptor   "Let the buyer beware."

de facto   actual, in reality

deus ex machina   a contrived, improbable agent which solves a situation

Dies Irae   Judgment Day

ex officio   by virtue of office or position

ipso facto   by the very fact

magnum opus   masterpiece

non sequitur   an illogical statement that doesn't "follow" what was just said

pro forma   as a matter of form or custom

quid pro quo   an exact exchange or substitution

quod erat demonstratum (**Q.E.D.**)   which was to be demonstrated or proved

sine die   indefinitely

sine qua non   an essential part or condition

Abbreviations to Remember

It's not just words alone that you'll encounter in your reading and writing. Here's a list of common abbreviations and special terms you will want to know.

a.k.a.   also known as

a.m.   (*ante meridiem*) before noon

A.W.O.L.   Absent Without Official Leave

bldg.   building

blvd.   boulevard

ca. (c.)   (*circa*) about

cf.   compare

C.O.D.   Cash On Delivery

db   decibel

d.b.a.   doing business as

e.g.   (*exempli gratia*) for example

et. al.   (*et alii*) and others

f., ff.   and the following page(s)

hp.   horsepower

ibid.   (*ibidem*) in the same place

i.e.   (*id est*) that is (to say)

loc. cit.   (*loco citato*) in the place cited

M   one thousand

ms., mss.   manuscript(s)

n.b.   (*nota bene*) take notice

op. cit.   (*opere citato*) in the work cited

p.m.   (*post meridiem*) after noon

p., pp.   page(s)

pro tem   (*pro tempore*) temporarily

p.s.i.   pound per square inch

r.p.m.   revolutions per minute

viz   namely

vs.   (*versus*) as against, in contrast to

French Terms to Remember

Whether in the world of fashion or in the "fashionable" world, French words and phrases are a natural element of conversation. Although these words still retain their French spellings and pronunciations, they are treated as essential parts of the English language.

à la carte   "from the menu", priced separately

avant-garde   at the forefront of a field; ahead of the times

bête noire   "black beast"; something you especially dislike or avoid

blasé   bored from overindulgence

bon mot   clever saying

bon vivant   one who enjoys the "good life" of luxury

bonhomie   good natured

bourgeois   middle-class

cause célèbre   a popular cause or issue

coiffure   hairstyle

cordon bleu   blue ribbon

coup de grace   "stroke of mercy"; the final blow

cul-de-sac   a dead end

denouement   unraveling or solution of a play or book's plot

détente   a relaxing or easing of relations

divertissement a diversion or amusement

éclat brilliant achievement

élan flair, style

en passant in passing; by the way

entrepreneur an adventurous business person

fait accompli an accomplished fact

faux pas "false step", a socially embarrassing mistake

fin de siècle turn-of-the-century

gauche "left-handed"; clumsy, inept

impasse a dead end or dilemma

ingenue an innocent, naive young woman

insousiance carefree indifference

laissez-faire noninterference

malaise a vague feeling of illness or depression

mélange a mixture

mot juste the appropriate thing to say

noblesse oblige the honorable behavior expected of high birth or rank

nom de plume pen-name, pseudonym

nouveau riche one who suddenly and ostentatiously has wealth

par excellence the epitome of something

parvenu a sudden newcomer to the upper class

pâtisserie bakery

pièce de résistance an outstanding accomplishment

piquant spicy, pungent

rapprochement a formal reconciliation

repartee a swift, witty reply

rêpondez s'il vous plait (R.S.V.P.) please reply

sangfroid "cold blood"; dispassionate, cool-headed

savoir faire tact, skill at always doing the proper thing

soupçon a trace; suspicion

tête-à-tête "head-to-head"; intimate meeting

tour de force feat of strength or brilliance

vignette a sketch or scene

Musical Terms to Remember

Did you ever look at a musical score and wonder what all those Italian words in the margins meant? Next time you "read" music, it will have a totally different meaning.

a cappella without accompaniment

adagio slow

agitato agitated

allegro lively, fast

alto low female voice (high male equivalent)

andante moving steadily

aria operatic song

arpeggio broken chord

basso low male voice

bravura technically difficult

cantibile flowing and lyrical

cantata work for chorus and orchestra

capriccio spirited

coda concluding section

con brio with spirit

concerto work for solo instrument and orchestra

crescendo becoming louder

diminuendo becoming quieter

dolce sweetly

falsetto very high male voice

finale final movement

forte loud

fortissimo very loud

intermezzo short interlude

largo slow

legato smooth

lento slow

missa Mass

pianissimo very soft

piano soft

poco a little

presto fast

scherzo lively movement in 3/4 time

sempre always

sonata composition for piano and/or solo instrument

soprano high female voice

staccato abrupt, short notes

tempo speed

tutti all

vivace lively

voce voice

Culinary Terms to Remember

Reading the ingredients of a foreign dish can be very confusing, but even menus written in English will sometimes use terms that mystify non-cooks. Here is a *baker's dozen* (13) of such terms describing methods of food preparation and serving.

al fresco   "outdoors"

bouquet garni   a mixture of finely chopped herbs, usually bay leaf, celery, thyme, and chervil, tied in a small cotton bag and added to cooking food

braise   to cook a browned roast in a covered pot at low temperature using very little liquid

en croûte   baked in pastry crust

en papillote   meat or fish wrapped in oil-coated paper and baked in its own juices

flambé   food coated with liquor and lit before serving

florentine   served with spinach

fines herbes   a mixture of finely chopped herbs, usually chervil, tarragon, basil, thyme, and lemon rind

julienne   cut in long, thin strips

sauté   to cook quickly in a small amount of butter and oil over a high flame

shirred   eggs baked and served in flat, shallow pottery dishes

tempura   Japanese style of deep-frying foods dipped in a thin batter

Véronique   a garnish of cooked seedless green grapes

Challenges 39–42: Vocabulary Around the World

As an experienced traveler, you should have no trouble matching the appropriate term in the right-hand column to its English "translation" in the left-hand column.

Challenge 39

1.	adagio	a.	noninterference
2.	fait accompli	b.	trace, suspicion
3.	al fresco	c.	spicy, pungent
4.	bon mot	d.	something disliked, avoided
5.	coda	e.	an accomplished fact
6.	soupçon	f.	outdoors
7.	laissez-faire	g.	concluding section
8.	piquant	h.	slow
9.	en passant	i.	clever saying
10.	bête noire	j.	by the way

Challenge 40

1.	legato	a.	relaxing or easing
2.	forte	b.	vague illness or depression
3.	bourgeois	c.	served with cooked grapes
4.	éclat	d.	swift, witty reply
5.	malaise	e.	bakery
6.	Véronique	f.	loud
7.	détente	g.	middle-class
8.	repartee	h.	cool-headedness
9.	pâtisserie	i.	brilliant achievement
10.	sangfroid	j.	smooth

Challenge 41

1.	crescendo	a.	naive young woman
2.	mot juste	b.	mixture
3.	savoir faire	c.	becoming louder
4.	ingenue	d.	cut in strips
5.	denouement	e.	appropriate thing to say
6.	insouciance	f.	flair
7.	julienne	g.	final movement
8.	mélange	h.	tact
9.	élan	i.	solution of plot
10.	finale	j.	carefree indifference

Challenge 42

1.	parvenu	a.	lively
2.	impasse	b.	reconciliation
3.	divertissement	c.	dilemma
4.	vivace	d.	clumsy
5.	faux pas	e.	served with spinach
6.	staccato	f.	an amusement
7.	gauche	g.	social newcomer
8.	vignette	h.	social mistake
9.	rapprochement	i.	abrupt, sharp notes
10.	florentine	j.	sketch or scene

Specialized Vocabularies

As intimidating and foreign as a doctor's vocabulary may sound to all of us, the language he or she uses when diagnosing an illness or injury is actually extremely simple. The words used in the scientific community are composed of very precise Greek word elements which, when understood, describe perfectly the condition or process in question. You don't have to have an M.D. to figure them out, either.

Just as was done with the word elements given in the earlier chapters, these common Greek word elements are presented in both a clustered format and then in an alphabetical listing, along with many common medical terms and expressions.

Likewise, the words and phrases used in the legal profession come to us from foreign sources, primarily Latin and French. These, too, are listed and defined.

The Word Elements of Science and Medicine

SUFFIXES

-ectomy	removal of
-ia	condition
-iasis	diseased
-in (-ine)	chemical substance
-itis (-itic)	inflammation
-oma	swelling
-osis (-otic)	diseased
-pathy	disease or treatment of
-rrhea (-rrhage)	discharge
-therapy	treatment

ROOTS

Characteristics

brachy	short	hyper	high
brady	slow	hypo	low
ecto	outer	scler	hard
endo	inner	tachy	fast

Colors

chlor	green	leuko	white
chrom	color	melan	black
cyan	blue	poli	gray
erythr	red	xanth	yellow

Parts of the Body

aden	gland	hyster	womb
angi	vein	larng	nose
arthr	joint	mast	breast
bronch	windpipe	my	muscle
card	heart	myel	marrow
cephal	head	myel	spinal cord
chir	hand	neph	kidney
chol	gall, bile	neuro	nerve
chondr	cartilage	opthalm	skull
crani	head, brain	oste	bone
cyst	bladder, sac	iti	eye
dactyl	finger, toe	pneu	lung, breath
derm	skin	phelb,	blood vessel
enter	intestine	ren	kidney
castr	stomach	rhin	nose
hem(em)	blood	stoma	mouth, opening
hepat	liver	trache	windpipe

Miscellaneous

alg	pain	mening	membrane
burs	sac	noia	mind
cyt	cell	pleg	paralysis
gangli	knot	psor	itch
glyc	sugar	psych	mind
hist	tissue	soma	body
lip	fat	tox	poison

---

aden- gland

alg- pain

allergist a doctor who treats allergies.

anesthesiologist a doctor who administers anesthesia.

anesthetist a specially trained nurse or technician who administers anesthesia.

aneurysm a dangerous bulging in a blood vessel.

ang- vein

angiogram a procedure used to reveal the condition of veins and arteries through X-rays of blood vessals injected with special dyes.

antibiotic   a group of chemical substances, such as penicillin, which retard the growth of or destory harmful bacteria.

arthr-   joint

benign   not dangerous

biopsy   surgical removal of tissue for microscopic examination

brachy-   short

brady-   slow

bronch-   windpipe (see **trache-**)

burs-   sac

carcinogenic   cancer-causing

carcinoma   a malignant tumor

card-   heart

cardiologist   a doctor who treats heart diseases.

cephal-   head, brain

chir-   hand

chlor-   green

chol-   gall, bile

chondr-   cartilage

chrom-   color

crani-   skull

cyan-   blue

cyst-   bladder; sac

cyt-   cell

dactyl-   finger, toe

derm-   skin

dermatologist   a doctor who treats skin disorders.

ecto-   outer

-ectomy   removal of (variant form **-tomy**)

EEG (Electroencephalogram)   a printed measurement of electrical activity in the brain (brain waves).

EKG (ECG, Electrocardiogram) a printed measurement of electrical activity in heart muscles used as a diagnostic tool in treating heart conditions.

endo- inner

endocrinologist a doctor who treats hormonal disorders.

enter- intestine

erythr- red

gangli- knot

gastr- stomach

gastroenterologist a doctor who treats disorders of the stomach and intestines.

GTT (Glucose Tolerance Test) a blood test which measures the amount of sugar in the diagnosis of diabetes (high blood sugar) or hypoglycemia (low blood sugar).

glyc- sugar

gynecologist a doctor who treats disorders of the female reproductive/sexual organs.

hem- blood (variant form **em-**)

hematologist a doctor who treats disorders of the blood and blood-producing organs.

hepat- liver

hepatologist a doctor who treats liver disorders.

hist- tissue

hyper- high

hypertension high blood pressure

hypo- low

hyster- womb

-ia condition

-iasis diseased

ICU Intensive Care Unit

-in chemical substance (variant form **-ine**)

intern a graduate of medical school receiving supervised hospital training.

internist a doctor who treats non-surgical disorders of the internal organs.

-itis   inflammation (variant form **-itic**)

-ium   part or lining of

laryng-   throat

leuko-   white

L.P.N. (Licensed Practical Nurse)   a non-diplomaed nurse trained in patient care.

lip-   fat

malignant   dangerous, deadly

mammography   an X-ray of the female breast.

mast-   breast

M.D. (Medical Doctor)   a graduate of medical school licensed to practice medicine.

melan-   black

mening-   membrane

metastasize   to spread from one part of the body to another

my-   muscle

myel- (1)   spinal cord

myel- (2)   marrow

M.I. (Myocardial Infarction)   a common form of heart attack, characterized by heart muscle damage due to lack of blood.

neph-   kidney (see **ren-**)

nephrologist   a doctor who treats kidney disorders.

neuro-   nerve

neurologist   a doctor who treats disorders of the nervous system.

noia-   mind (see **psych-**)

obstetrician   a doctor who treats women during pregnancy and childbirth.

-oma   swelling

ophthalm-   eye

ophthalmologist   a doctor who treats eye disorders.

orthopedist   a doctor who treats disorders of the musculo-skeletal system.

-osis   diseased (variant form **-otic**)

oste-   bone

oto- ear

otorhinolaryngologist a doctor who treats disorders of the ear, nose, and throat.

-pathy disease or treatment of

pathologist a doctor who diagnoses disease through tissue examination.

pediatrician a doctor who treats children.

pertussis whooping cough

phleb- blood vessel

pleg- paralysis

pneu- lung, breath

podiatrist a trained specialist (usually not an M.D.) who treats foot disorders.

poli- gray

proctologist a doctor who treats disorders of the colon, rectum, and anus.

psor- itch

psych- mind (see **noia-**)

psychiatrist a doctor who treats disorders of the mind.

pyrexia fever

resident a doctor who has completed his internship and is continuing hospital training in a specialty.

R.N. (Registered Nurse) a licensed graduate of an accredited school of nursing trained to care for the sick.

ren- kidney (see **neph-**)

rheumatologist a doctor who treats joint disorders.

rhin- nose

rhus dermatitis poison ivy

-rrhea discharge (variant form **-rrhage**)

rubella german measles

rubeolla measles

scler- hard

som- body

stoma- mouth, opening

surgeon a doctor specially trained to perform surgery.

syncope fainting

tachy- fast

-therapy treatment

tinea pedis athlete's foot

tox- poison

trache- windpipe (see **bronch-**)

varicella chicken pox

UA (Urinalysis) chemical analysis of urine for diagnostic purposes

urologist a doctor who treats disorders of the male sexual organs and urinary system.

xanth- yellow

Challenges 43–44: Medical Terminology

Using the Greek medical and scientific word elements you've just learned (and a few you should remember from the Building Blocks sections), match the following columns of words with their "translations."

Challenge 43

1. poisonous substance
2. abnormally short fingers
3. bruise; blood swelling
4. inflammation of the liver
5. abnormal discharge of blood
6. lining around the heart
7. diseased mind
8. ear, nose, and throat doctor
9. inflammation of stomach and intestines
10. diseased white blood cells
11. abnormally slow heartbeat
12. paralysis of four limbs
13. hardening of the arteries
14. brain wave measurement
15. bluish skin condition

a. bradycardia
b. otorhino-laryngologist
c. hematoma
d. psychotic
e. hepatitis
f. arteriosclerosis
g. leukemia
h. toxin

i. hemorrhage
j. brachydactylism
k. pericardium
l. cyanosis
m. encephalogram
n. gastroenteritis
o. quadraplegia

Challenge 44

1. endocarditis
2. hysterectomy
3. psoriasis
4. erythrocyte
5. neuralgia
6. hypoglycemia
7. histology
8. poliomyelitis
9. ophthalmologist
10. xanthoderma

a. red blood cell
b. eye doctor
c. nerve pain
d. yellowish skin
e. inflammation of gray spinal matter
f. inflammation of inner heart lining
g. diseased itching
h. low blood sugar
i. removal of womb
j. study of tissue cells

Challenge 45

Circle the word that best completes each sentence.

1. Her hay fever symptoms were so severe that she had to go to the _____ for shots.
   a. internist
   b. radiologist
   c. cardiologist
   d. allergist

2. A doctor who treats kidney disorders is a _____.
   a. hematologist
   b. neurologist
   c. nephrologist
   d. gynecologist

3. When he developed a fever from the infected wound, the doctors prescribed _____.
   a. mammography
   b. pertussis
   c. antibiotics
   d. biopsy

4. A doctor who treats women during pregnancy and childbirth is a _____.
   a. opthalmologist
   b. orthopedist
   c. optometrist
   d. obstetrician

5. She was greatly relieved to hear that the lump in her arm was _____, not malignant.
   a. carcinoma
   b. benign
   c. pyrexia
   d. aneurysm

6. A doctor who treats liver disorders is a _____.
   a. hepatologist
   b. herpetologist
   c. nephrologist
   d. anaesthesiologist

7. Certain chemical substances have been shown in laboratory experiments to cause cancer and are thus considered to be _____.
   a. antibiotic
   b. catatonic
   c. carcinogenic
   d. benign

8. A doctor who has completed an internship and is continuing hospital training in a specialty is called a _____.
   a. internist
   b. intern
   c. resident
   d. surgeon

9. After the _____ showed irregularities in his heartbeat, the doctor put him in the hospital for further testing.
   a. GTT
   b. ICU
   c. EEG
   d. EKG

10. A non-diplomaed nurse trained in patient care is a _____.
    a. ICU
    b. L.P.N.
    c. M.D.
    d. R.N.

The Language of Law

Whether signing a contract or writing a will, all of us need to understand the basic language of the legal profession. Here's a list of common terms you need to increase your command of the langauge.

abscond   to flee suddenly to avoid prosecution or arrest

accessory   a person who assists in a crime, while not participating in it

accomplice   one who knowingly participates in a crime

abjudication   a legal judgment or ruling

affidavit   a sworn written statement signed before an authorized officer of the court such as a notary public

altercation   a heated argument or noisy quarrel

amicus curiae (L. "friend of the court")   one who, although not involved in a lawsuit, has enough interest in its outcome to be allowed to present an argument or introduce evidence by way of an amicus brief.

appellate court   reviews cases and appeals pertaining to judgments reached by a trial court.

arraignment   formal court appearance of a defendant, after an indictment has been filed, where charges, rights, and pleas are presented

arson   the malicious setting afire of property

assault   an attempt or threat to inflict bodily harm on another person

barrister   a British lawyer who is admitted to plead cases before superior court

battery   unconsented use of physical force on another person

bequest   property given to someone in a will

codicil   a supplement or appendix to a will

collusion   secret cooperation with another person for improper or illegal purposes

contiguous   sharing a boundary; adjacent

contraband   goods prohibited by law or treaty to be imported or exported

contumacious   insubordinate or rebellious

corpus delicti (L. "the body of the crime")   the physical proof of a crime and criminal intent

defendant   the person or party sued by the plaintiff in civil lawsuits

deposition   a written record of a witness' sworn testimony before a trial

disenfranchise   to deprive of a right of citizenship, such as the right to vote

embezzlement   unauthorized use of funds of which one has lawful possession but not ownership

eminent domain   the government's right to take private land for public use with payment of just compensation

equity   an equitable right or claim; justice applied in circumstances not covered by law

exhume   to remove from a grave

ex post facto (L. "after the fact")   retroactive

extradition   the legal surrender of an alleged criminal to another jurisdiction for trial

felony   a serious crime punishable by imprisonment or death

fraud   intentional deceit or misrepresentation which cheats or harms another person

habeas corpus (L. "you have the body")   a court ordered writ demanding that a person being held in custody or imprisonment be brought before the court to determine the legality of the detainment

immaterial   irrelevent or inconsequential

incarcerate   to put in jail

indictment   the formal written criminal accusation needed by the grand jury to decide whether enough evidence exists to warrant a trial

injunction   a court order enjoining or prohibiting someone from a specific action

inquest   a court ordered investigation of facts in a criminal case

intestate   to die without leaving a will

jurisdiction   the legal authority and/or geographical territory of a particular court

jurisprudence   the science and philosophy of law

larceny   theft

libel   a printed or broadcast statement that is both false and damaging to someone's reputation

lien   a financial claim on a piece of property belonging to someone

litigation   disputes or issues that will be settled by a court of law

manslaughter   the unlawful killing of someone but without premeditation or malice

miscreant   an evildoer

misdemeanor   a relatively minor criminal offense usually punishable by a fine or short jail term

nolo contendere (L. "I do not wish to contend")   an acceptance of the facts in an indictment, as opposed to a formal plea of guilty, on which the judge would pass judgment

non compos mentis (L. "not of sound mind")   legally insane or incompetent

ordinance   law enacted by local authorities on matters of local concern

perjury   making a false statement under oath

perpetrator   one who commits a crime

pettifogger   a petty, unscrupulous lawyer

plagiarism   to use someone else's ideas or writings as one's own

plaintiff   the person or group initiating a civil lawsuit

probate   the procedure of determining the validity of a will and distributing the estate as indicated in the will

probation   a nonprison sentence sometimes given after a defendant has been found guilty

pro bono publico (L. "for the public good")   free legal representation for a beneficial cause

pro se (L. "for himself")   when a person represents himself in court rather than retaining a lawyer to represent him

retainer   the advance fee paid a lawyer for future services

shyster   an unethical lawyer

statute   a law enacted by federal or state legislation

subpoena (L. "under penalty")   a court ordered writ requiring a witness to attend a judicial proceeding

tort   a non-contract violation of civil law which damages or injures another

tribunal   a seat or court of justice

warrant   a written court order authorizing an act such as a search or an arrest

Challenge 46: The Language of the Law

Circle the word that best completes each sentence.

1. By the time the police arrived at the bank to question the employee suspected of embezzlement, he had _____ with $5,000.00.
   a. exhumed   c. absconded
   b. assaulted   d. deposed

2. The prosecutors were looking for the _____ who had provided the car used in the hold-up.
   a. defendant   c. accomplice
   b. accessory   d. shyster

3. The defendant stood before the judge during the _____ and listened carefully to the charges against him.
   a. arraignment
   b. injunction
   c. indictment
   d. subpoena

4. The television reporter wanted the actress charged with _____ for pushing him down the stairs.
   a. altercation
   b. arson
   c. battery
   d. manslaughter

5. When the Coast Guard inspected the abandoned boat, they found that the smugglers had left behind most of the _____ during their hasty escape.
   a. contraband   c. statute
   b. equity   d. lien

6. Only a professional surveyor can determine the exact boundary of _____ pieces of property.
   a. contumacious
   b. intestate
   c. probate
   d. contiguous

7. The consumer _____ division of the attorney general's office tries to protect innocent people from the deceptive promises and defective products of unscrupulous salesmen.
   a. litigation   c. tort
   b. fraud   d. larceny

8. When you take out a loan to purchase a new car, the bank has a _____ on the car.
   a. fraud   c. libel
   b. inquest   d. lien

9. The convicted criminal was _____ at the federal prison.
   a. incarcerated   c. extradited
   b. indicted   d. intestate

10. To be legally insane or incompetent is to be _____.
    a. *nolo contendere*
    b. *pro bono publico*
    c. *non compos mentis*
    d. *corpus delicti*

Part III

WORDS TO WATCH

When is it correct to use *accompanied with* as opposed to *accompanied by*? What's the difference in meaning between *cannon* and *canon*? Why is it incorrect to use *anticipate* when you mean *expect*? Is that word spelled *beseige* or *besiege*?

Having a powerful command of vocabulary demands precise and skillful use of such fine points of expression in both verbal and written communication. The aim of this book is to give you all the ammunition you need for maximum command of the language. The following Correct Usage Master List includes common examples of these fine points, such as troublesome words, spelling, synonyms, and verb/preposition pairs. It is followed by challenging exercises to test your progress in building a power vocabulary.

Correct Usage Master List

A

ability (skill) *vs.* capacity (aptitude)

> After so many years of studying piano, he has the *ability* to play even the most difficult compositions.
> We all have the *capacity* to love our fellow man.

abstain *from*

> People with certain kinds of heart disease must *abstain from* eating fatty foods.

accede *to*

> They will *accede to* our request and allow us to use their research documents.

accompanied *with* (*referring to objects*) *vs.* accompanied *by* (*referring to persons*)

> He was a well-equipped hunter, *accompanied with* several rifles and plenty of ammunition.
> Whenever the duchess paid a visit to our city, she was *accompanied by* her personal physician.

73

(in) accordance *with*

> The student agreed to submit extra work *in accordance with* the professor's request.

accountable *for* (*referring to actions*) *vs.* **accountable** *to* (*referring to persons*)

> Although the judge acknowledged the boy's youth, she decreed that he should be held *accountable for* his crimes.
>
> You will be *accountable to* your immediate supervisor if you fail to complete the project.

acheive *Incorrect.* Spell it *achieve.*

> Remember: *I* E*x*cel.

adverse to (unfavorable) *vs.* **averse to** (reluctant)

> She was *adverse to* the idea of marrying the old man her parents chose for her, in spite of their pleas.
>
> I am *averse to* getting involved in any money scheme that promises to make me rich overnight.

advice (noun, wise suggestion) *vs.* **advise** (verb, to counsel)

> My uncle was always full of good *advice* about finances.
> She *advised* me to eat fewer fatty foods.

affect (to influence or change) *vs.* **effect** (verb, to bring about; noun, result)

> The bad weather will not *affect* my plans.
> We must *effect* a solution to this chronic problem once and for all.
> The *effects* of your behavior may not appear to be serious to you, but many other people will be upset.

aggravate (to make worse) *vs.* **irritate** (to annoy)

> Eating that pepperoni pizza is certain to *aggravate* your ulcer.
> His constant interruptions began to *irritate* the speaker.

aid (assistance) *vs.* **aide** (assistant)

> After the earthquake struck, many countries donated *aid* in the form of tents, emergency medical supplies, and food.
> The general was assisted by his *aide* during the award ceremony.

allusion (*an indirect reference*) *vs.* **reference** (*a direct mention*)

> The image of the apple in this painting is a subtle *allusion* to the story of Adam and Eve.
> He frequently made *reference* to great scholars, quoting long passages from famous journals.

allusion (*an indirect reference*) *vs.* illusion (*false idea or unreal image*)

> She made an *allusion* to the Bible when she spoke of the Good Book.
> The shimmering heat created the *illusion* of water on the highway.

aloof *from*

> She held herself *aloof from* the rest of the crowd, preferring to be by herself.

alright *Incorrect.* Use *all right.*

altar (a religious platform) *vs.* alter (to change)

> The villagers placed their offerings of fruit and bread to the gods on the *altar.*
> We cannot *alter* the course of hurricanes.

ambiguous (not clear, vague, unintentionally confusing) *vs.* equivocal (purposely vague, intentionally confusing)

> He regretted that his carelessness produced an *ambiguous* report which left everyone confused.
> The salesman soon had the couple signing the contract, unaware of his *equivocal* promises.

among (*referring to more than two*) *vs.* between (*referring to two*)

> We distributed the money *among* the five children.
> Just *between* you and me, I think it's going to rain during the barbecue.

anticipate (to expect and prepare for) *vs.* expect (to look forward to)

> We've stocked up on plenty of food, as we *anticipate* a lot of spur-of-the-moment visitors over the holiday.
> She *expected* a raise at the end of the year.

anxious (uneasy, apprehensive, worried) *vs.* eager (feeling keen desire, impatient to do or get)

> The thought of having to go to the dentist made her extremely *anxious.*
> We were *eager* to meet our son's fiancée.

apathy *toward*

> A depressed person shows *apathy toward* even happy events or news.

assent *to*

> I will *assent to* your requests and provide the documents you need.

assume (to take for granted, suppose) *vs.* presume (to accept as true, lacking proof to the contrary)

> I *assume* he'd have the foresight to investigate the money deal thoroughly before signing the contract.
> I *presume* all people enjoy weddings.

avenge (to punish justly) *vs.* revenge (to retaliate)

> The young man vowed to *avenge* his father's death and find the murderers.
> Even though the criminal was behind bars, the victim plotted *revenge*, planning to wait ten years if necessary.

B

badmitton *Incorrect.* Spell it *badminton.*

bate (to lessen force of) *vs.* bait (to lure, tease, torment)

> His temper was *bated* by her soft words.
> We *baited* the fishing hook with minnows.

being as *Incorrect.* Use *seeing as.*

beseige *Incorrect.* Spell it *besiege.*

> Remember: *Soldiers In Every Gate.*

beside (at the side of) *vs.* besides (in addition to)

> The loyal dog lay down *beside* his master.
> *Besides* going to the theater, we plan to stop at the museum.

bloc (alliance) *vs.* block (a cube)

> The Communist *bloc* of Eastern Europe includes Poland and East Germany.
> The sundial sat on a *block* of granite.

blow, blew, have blown

> I *blow* the horn.
> Yesterday I *blew* the horn.
> In the past, I *have blown* the horn.

bring (*to me*) *vs.* take (*from me*)

> When you come to visit me this afternoon, please *bring* that book you borrowed.
> When you leave, *take* your coat with you.

burst, burst, have burst

> A container *bursts* if overfilled.
> I heard that your waterpipes *burst* last night.
> Dams *have burst* in years past—before modern engineering produced safer designs.

bust *Incorrect.* Use *burst*.

C

callus (painful growth on foot) *vs.* callous (lacking pity, insensitive)

> If you wear shoes that are too tight, you might develop a *callus* on your foot.
> A *callous* person seems not to notice the suffering of his fellow man.

cannon (weapon) *vs.* canon (law or rule)

> The small children were startled and began to cry when the *cannon* went off.
> According to the religious order's *canon*, no one was allowed to eat meat or drink alcohol.

canvas (heavy cloth) *vs.* canvass (to examine in detail or survey)

> Because it had rained the night before, we spread a *canvas* on the ground before we sat down to our picnic.
> The researchers were required to *canvass* the neighborhood about people's choices in the upcoming elections.

capital (money; chief) *vs.* capitol (building)

> You need a great deal of *capital* to start a new business.
> The *capital* cause of this problem is poverty.
> We visted the *Capitol* and the White House when we went to Washington, D.C.

caution *against*

> The Surgeon General cautions *against* smoking cigarettes, especially during pregnancy.

ceremonial (*pertaining to things*) *vs.* ceremonious (*pertaining to both things and people*)

> The chief wore his *ceremonial* robes to impress the villagers.
> You needn't be so *ceremonious* with me; I'm perfectly happy with the Thanksgiving leftovers.

cite (to refer to) *vs.* **site** (location)

> To prove his point, the young man *cited* several instances as examples.
> We hauled the lumber to the building *site*.

coincide *with*

> It's always a good idea to have your loan payment date *coincide with* payday.

commiserate *with*

> The students who failed the entrance examination *commiserated with* each other over coffee.

compare *to* (*pertaining to similarities*) *vs.* **compare** *with* (*pertaining to both similarities and differences*)

> Let's *compare* this broken latch *to* the new one to make sure it'll fit the door.
> The teacher gave the same test each week to a different class to see how the classes *compared with* one another.

complacent (self-satisfied, smug) *vs.* **complaisant** (willing to please, obliging)

> You should never become *complacent* about how valuable you are to the company.
> The *complaisant* child offered to run the errands.

complement (that which completes) *vs.* **compliment** (an expression of courtesy or respect)

> Your gold scarf and brown coat are perfect *complements* for your reddish hair.
> The guests *complimented* the hostess on the superb dinner she had served.

comprise (to include, consist of; *parts embracing whole*) *vs.* **composed** *of* (to make up or constitute; *whole embracing parts*)

> Four movements *comprise* the typical symphony.
> The typical symphony is *composed* of four movements.

concensus of opinion *Incorrect* Use *consensus*.

conducive *to*

> Eating fruits and whole-grain foods is *conducive to* good health.

consists *of* (to be formed or composed of parts) *vs.* **consists** *in* (to be inherent in something)

> The procedure *consists of* six steps.
> The meaning of life *consists in* loving one's fellow man and woman under all circumstances.

continual (happening over and over, at intervals) *vs.* continuous (going on uninterrupted)

> Although he had his good days, his *continual* tantrums wore his parents out.
> The *continuous* hum of the engine made the bus driver sleepy.

contrast *to* (*pertaining to opposites*) *vs.* contrast *with* (*pertaining to differences*)

> She is a model employee, in *contrast to* her predecessor, whom we fired.
> The yellow blouse was a pleasing *contrast with* the brown shirt.

councilor (member of council) *vs.* counselor (one who counsels, gives advice)

> My uncle's greatest personal victory was winning his bid for city *councilor* after a long and exhausting campaign.
> When the elderly couple won the lottery, they wisely sought the advice of a financial *counselor* on how best to use their money.

crisis (s.), crises (pl.)

criterion (s.), criteria (pl.)

cynical (sarcastic, sneering) *vs.* skeptical (not easily persuaded, doubting)

> The disillusioned and *cynical* employee had nothing but criticism to offer about his boss.
> The *skeptical* customer was not entirely convinced of the salesman's promises.

D

defendent *Incorrect.* Spell it *defendant.*

> Remember: A defend*ant* *ant*icipates a verdict.

definite (precise and clear in meaning) *vs.* definitive (decisive, conclusive)

> The sound of the explosion was *definitely* coming from the east.
> After months of research and interviews, the reporter filed a *definitive* story on how the scandal had begun.

denote (to refer to explicitly) *vs.* connote (to suggest or imply)

> The *denotation* of the word *bread* is simply a loaf of baked dough.
> The *connotation* of bread, however, could mean "money" to a teenager, or "security" to a hungry man.

deprive *of*

> The Constitution forbids the government to *deprive* citizens *of* their right to free speech.

desist *from*

> The speaker pleaded with the audience to *desist from* throwing bottles on the stage.

despair *of*

> Until the dog appeared at the front door, the child had *despaired of* seeing it again.

destitute *of*

> In drought-stricken lands, the people are *destitute of* the water they need to grow their crops.

deviate *from*

> The procedures are extremely precise and clear; you must not *deviate from* them in any way.

different *from* (pertaining to direct contrast) *vs.* different *than* (pertaining to degrees of difference)

> My opinions may be *different from* those of everyone else, but it is my right to speak my mind.
> As hard as it is to believe, Mary's way of handling money is even more *different than* her brother Robert's is to ours.

differs *from* (*pertaining to dissimilarities*) *vs.* differs *with* (*pertaining to a disagreement*)

> The taste of broiled chicken *differs* greatly *from* that of stewed chicken.
> I find it difficult to work with him; we *differ with* each other on every issue we confront.

discreet (prudent, careful) *vs.* discrete (separate and distinct)

> So as not to embarrass the hostess, the man made a *discreet* remark about the tear in her dress.
> Although the chemical reaction is quite rapid, you can observe four *discrete* stages in the process.

discourage *from*

> It's really none of my busines, but I would *discourage* you *from* saying that in front of the children.

disinterested (impartial, unbiased) *vs.* uninterested (indifferent)

> Every person accused of a crime hopes to be tried by a *disinterested* judge.
> After sitting through the first hour of that terrible movie, I was *uninterested* in staying for the ending.

dissimilar *to*

> The rates for your new insurance policy have gone up because your new car is *dissimilar to* your previous car in many ways.

divest *of*

> When he decided to join the priesthood, he left behind his possessions and *divested* himself *of* his wealth.

drink, drank, have drunk

> I *drink* apple juice everyday.
> I *drank* champagne at my sister's wedding last year.
> I *have drunk* tea before, but I've never liked the taste.

E

egoism (self-interested, self-centered) *vs.* egotism (constant reference to self)

> His *egoism* irritates his co-workers because he won't help anyone unless there's some benefit in doing so for himself.
> No one is interested in listening to the bragging and name-dropping of an *egotistical* person.

elder (*referring to persons*) *vs.* older (*referring to things*)

> My *elder* brother is thirty-six; my eldest is forty-two.
> *Older* homes are often not insulated properly.

emanate *from*

> In the weak light of dawn, we could see the light from the burning building *emanating from* the valley.

embarasment *Incorrect.* Spell it *embarrassment.*

> Remember: *Really Red* for *Silly Statements.*

emigrate *from*

> His grandparents had *emigrated from* Puerto Rico in hopes of a better life for their children.

enhance (to highlight) *vs.* improve (to make better)

> Her bright lipstick *enhanced* her beautiful teeth.
> You need to study harder and longer if you want to *improve* your grades.

enthralled *by*

> The children were *enthralled by* the magician's tricks and mysterious chants.

enthused *Incorrect.* Use *enthusiastic.*

enviroment *Incorrect.* Spell it *environment.*

> Remember: There's *iron* in the env*iron*ment.

envy (discontent or resentment because of someone else's advantage) *vs.* jealousy (suspicion of rivalry)

> It does you no good to *envy* her promotion and raise; she's been here five years longer than you.
> It's unfortunate that there's only one position open; there are three qualified candidates, and there's bound to be *jealousy* among them now.

exclude *from*

> Only people with perfect driving records will be allowed into the program; all others will be *excluded from* it.

F

farther (*pertaining to distance*) *vs.* further (*pertaining to time or degree*)

> As his broken foot healed, he was able to walk *farther* each day.
> We can pursue the issue *further* at our next meeting.

feasible (capable of being done) *vs.* possible (capable of existing or happening)

> If we have enough time, it's *feasible* that we can repair the leak completely.
> People who live in California are aware that a major earthquake is *possible* at any time.

fewer (*referring to number*) *vs.* less (*referring to amount*)

> There were *fewer* people in the lecture hall after the intermission.
> After the hurricane, there was *less* sand blocking the channel.

flaunt (to make a conspicuous or defiant display) *vs.* flout (to mock or scoff at, to show contempt for)

> Only fools *flaunt* their gold jewelry in a high-crime area.
> She thought nothing of *flouting* the traffic laws; she threw away every parking ticket she found on her windshield.

forebear (ancestor) *vs.* forbear (to endure, tolerate)

> Our *forebears* settled this territory over three hundred years ago.
> She showed great *forbearance* in dealing with such difficult clients.

forbid, forbade, have forbidden.

> We *forbid* minors to drink here.
> He *forbade* the children to play in the street.
> They *have forbidden* foreigners to leave the country until the crisis has been resolved.

former *(that mentioned first)* vs. latter *(that mentioned second)*

> The doctors advised him that either the infection would clear up on its own, or it would spread rapidly. If the *former* happened, he would no longer need the medication; if the *latter*, he would need surgery immediately.

forward (moving ahead) vs. foreword (an introductory remark, preface)

> We had to push the Jeep out of the mud before we could move *forward*.
> The author wrote a *foreword* to the second edition of his controversial book, explaining why he felt the position he had taken in it was justified.

founder (to stumble or sink) vs. flounder (to struggle or speak awkwardly)

> The ship *foundered* rapidly when its keel was ruptured by the rocks.
> The fish *floundered* desperately on the deck of the sailboat.

G

gourmet (a person who is an excellent judge of fine foods and drinks, epicure) *vs.* gourmand (a person with a hearty appetite in excess)

> A true *gourmet* would never serve red wine with chicken.
> Only a *gourmand* would make five trips to the buffet table.

goverment *Incorrect.* Spell it *government*.

> Remember: govern, governor, government

graduate *from*

> I *graduated from* Ashland High School in 1981.

grateful *to (referring to person)* vs. grateful *for (referring to things)*

> I am *grateful to* you for all the help you gave me when I started working here.
> The school principal was *grateful for* the computer our company donated.

H

hanged *(pertaining to a person)* vs. hung *(pertaining to an object)*

> The convicted murderer was sentenced to be *hanged*.
> We *hung* the mirror above the fireplace.

homogeneous (similar or identical) *vs.* homogenous (similar in structure, uniform)

> The skeletal structure of a parrot and a chicken are *homogeneous.*
> When the fat content of raw milk is evenly distributed, the milk is said to be *homogenous* or to have been homogenized.

hygeine *Incorrect.* Spell it *hygiene.*

> Remember: Cleanliness *Is* Essential.

I

imminent (impending) *vs.* eminent (lofty, distinguished, outstanding)

> The coastal areas were evacuated after the Weather Service warned of an *imminent* hurricane.
> All the doctors wanted to work with such an *eminent* surgeon.

imply (to hint, suggest) *vs.* infer (to conclude, deduce)

> I did not *imply* you were lazy when I said you hadn't helped me out, for I knew you weren't feeling well that day.
> We can *infer* from his remarks that there's a lot going on that we don't know about.

incredible (unbelievable) *vs.* incredulous (unbelieving)

> It was an *incredible* feat of strength for a young child to move that couch.
> The people laughed at the politician's promise to balance the budget; such a wild plan would only get an *incredulous* response.

infuse *with*

> The pale liquid was *infused with* a red dye that turned it pinkish.

ingenious (clever, inventive) *vs.* ingenuous (open, candid, without guile)

> Repairing that torn curtain with a paper clip was an *ingenious* solution.
> The *ingenuous* girl truly believed that a new hairstyle would make her more alluring.

insight *into*

> After listening to how the two people conversed, he had a clear *insight into* why they didn't get along.

inundate *with*

> As soon as we announced our intention to marry, we were *inundated with* cards and gifts.

irregardless *Incorrect.* Use *regardless.*

J

judgement *Incorrect.* Spell it *judgment.*

 Remember: Only the English add *E.*

justified *in*

 I feel that I am *justified in* taking this step; there are no viable alternatives.

L

lacking *in*

 An impetuous person is *lacking in* patience and foresight.

lay (takes an object) *vs.* lie (does not take an object)

 I *lay* bricks. I *laid* bricks yesterday. I *have laid* bricks in years past.
 I *lie* down when I'm tired. I *lay* down yesterday when I got tired. I *have lain* down whenever I felt tired.

liason *Incorrect.* Spell it *liaison.*

 Remember: *It's Always Icy.*

like it was (used in informal speech) *vs.* as if it were (used in formal speech)

 The car made a strange noise, *like it was* ready to conk out.
 The bird hovered over the pool, *as if it were* deciding to plunge in or not.

loath (unwilling, reluctant) *vs.* loathe (to feel intense dislike, disgust, to detest)

 I am *loath* to choose the winner, seeing as three people had the correct answer. I *loathe* having to talk to that cruel man about how he treats his dog, but someone must defend that poor creature.

loose *vs.* lose

 Remember: The n*oo*se is l*oo*se. What you l*o*se is a l*o*ss.

M

marred *by*

 The once-beautiful table had been *marred by* years of careless use.

medium (s.), media (pl.)

miniscule *Incorrect.* Spell it *minuscule.*
 Remember: There's *minus* in *minus*cule.

N

nauseous (sickening, disgusting) *vs.* **nauseated** (to feel sick)

> The smell of rotting garbage is *nauseous*.
> She was *nauseated* after the roller-coaster ride.

noisome (harmful, foul-smelling) *vs.* **noisy** (loud)

> Whatever he's cooking has a horrible, *noisome* odor.
> The classroom was filled with *noisy*, playful children.

O

opposition *to*

> They were in *opposition to* any law that restricted their access to the river.

orientate *Incorrect.* Use *orient*.

P

parameter (a constant) *vs.* **perimeter** (an outer boundary)

> We have to finish this job within the *parameters* of a fixed budget and a tight schedule.
> They planted spruce trees along the *perimeter* of the property.

perquisite (a tip, privilege, benefit) *vs.* **prerequisite** (something required beforehand)

> A limitless expense account is a *perquisite* of the chairman's position.
> A high school diploma is a *prerequisite* of the job.

persevere *in*

> As difficult as it may seem, you must *persevere in* your therapy if you want to play tennis again.

perspective (a specific viewpoint) *vs.* **prospective** (expected, future)

> The situation may seem disastrous to you, but if you look at it from my *perspective*, you'll see that it presents us with a unique challenge.
> Salespeople are always trained to regard all contacts as *prospective* clients.

pertinent *to*

> This discussion is really not *pertinent to* the main subject.

pertinent (relevant) *vs.* pertaining (associated with, relative to)

> She made some very *pertinent* remarks about our plan after having read the report we wrote.
> *Pertaining* to the weather, air pollution plays a significant role.

phenomenon (s.), phenomena (pl.)

precipitate (to bring on, to hasten) *vs.* precipitous (steep)

> Such foolhardy plans will *precipitate* a major crisis.
> Be very careful when you drive along that route; there are several *precipitous* drops and cliffs on the way down.

preclude (to make impossible or unnecessary) *vs.* prevent (to stop from happening)

> Your having brought the refreshments *precludes* our having to go out and buy them now.
> This vaccine will *prevent* a recurrence of the disease.

principal (first in rank, authority, importance) *vs.* principle (fundamental truth or law)

> The *principal* cause of the disease is contaminated water.
> It is a *principle* of our society that all people are created equal.

proceed (to advance, to move forward) *vs.* precede (to come before)

> Now that we have all the supplies we need for the coming trip, we can *proceed* as planned.
> It is important that a thorough washing *precedes* all applications of the medication.

proved (tested conclusively) *vs.* proven (tested by time)

> After several successful experiments, his theory was *proved* true.
> Chicken soup has *proven* effective in relieving the symptoms of the common cold.

publicity (*has a positive connotation*) *vs.* notoriety (*has a negative connotation*)

> Donating money to a charity can bring needed *publicity* to a new politician; cheating on his taxes would certainly bring *notoriety*.

punishable *by*

> Public drunkenness is *punishable by* thirty days in the county jail.

R

raise *(takes an object)* *vs.* **rise** *(does not take an object)*

We *raised* the beam over our heads and carried it to the work site.
Please *rise* when the judge enters.

redolent *of*

The kitchen was *redolent of* the aromas of Thanksgiving dinner.

reign (ruler's tenure on throne) *vs.* **rein** (leather strap)

The young prince's *reign* began with an elaborate ceremony.
The cowboy pulled hard on the horse's *rein* to avoid the oncoming herd.

replete *with*

The stockroom was overflowing, *replete with* unsold inventory.

repulse (to drive back) *vs.* **repel** (to disgust)

They successfully *repulsed* the oncoming army by using mortars.
The woman were *repelled* by the waiter's filthy hands.

reticent (silent, disinclined to talk) *vs.* **reluctant** (unwilling)

The young girl was *reticent*, unsure of her skills in English.
I am *reluctant* to point a finger of blame at anyone, seeing as I did not see what happened.

revel *in*

In the autumn, children and adults alike *revel in* jumping into piles of raked leaves.

rhythym *Incorrect. Spell it* rhythm.

Remember: *Have You Timed His Music?*

ring, rang, have rung

I *ring* the doorbell.
I *rang* the chimes at church yesterday.
I *have rung* churchbells in the past.

rise, rose, have risen

I *rise* from my chair.
I *rose* from bed in spite of my fever.
I *had risen* too quickly and felt dizzy as a result.

S

sacreligious *Incorrect.* Spell it *sacrilegious.*

> Remember: There's no *religi*on in sacri*legi*ous.

satiate *with*

> The children fell asleep quickly, *satiated with* plum puddings and Christmas tarts.

seek, sought, have sought

> You should *seek* medical help for that bleeding.
> I *sought* the owner of the umbrella I found.
> We *have sought* security and comfort.

sensual (connected with sexual pleasure) *vs.* sensuous (appealing to the senses)

> At her shower, the bride-to-be is often given *sensual* nightgowns.
> He loved the *sensuous* texture of suede.

seperate *Incorrect.* Spell it *separate.*

> Remember: Se*pa*rate the *pa*rts.

should of *Incorrect.* Use *should have.*

sieze *Incorrect.* Spell it *seize.*

> Remember: *S*natch *E*very *I*nch.

sing, sang, have sung

> I always *sing* in the shower.
> We *sang* Happy Birthday to her last night.
> We *have sung* many times at the church.

stationary (not moving, standing still) *vs.* stationery (writing papers)

> Although the truck was *stationary*, we knew it would roll down the hill if we didn't keep the fallen log in front of the wheels.
> My grandmother uses her cream-colored *stationery* to write thank-you notes.

straight (not crooked) *vs.* strait (difficulty, distress)

> In order for the table to be level, it's important that the legs be even and *straight.*
> The inhabitants of the village were in dire *straits* after the tornado swept through.

stratum (s.), strata (pl.)

swim, swam, have swum

> It is important that you learn to *swim*.
> When he was only nineteen, he *swam* the English Channel.
> We *have swum* across the river every summer.

swing, swung, have swung

> I want the pendulum to *swing* freely.
> When we released the knob, the door *swung* open.
> They *have swung* that rope so many times there's a mark on the sidewalk from it.

T

temperment *Incorrect.* Spell it *temperament*.

> Remember: There's *a temper* in *temper*ament.

that (*used in a restrictive phrase*) *vs.* which (*used in a nonrestrictive phrase*)

> The house *that* we wanted to buy had already been sold by the time we got to the real estate agent's office.
> The grandfather clock, *which* chimes every hour, is in the repair shop for two more weeks.

tortuous (full of twists and turns, winding) *vs.* torturous (very painful)

> The mountain trails were so steep and *tortuous* that no cars were allowed on them.
> A root canal is a *torturous* procedure if performed without anesthesia.

toward (*American usage*) *vs.* towards (*British usage*)

turbid (muddy, clouded, confused) *vs.* turgid (swollen)

> The pond was *turbid* and filled with fallen leaves after the storm.
> The cooked sausages were *turgid* and ready to burst.

try and *Incorrect.* Use *try to*.

U

unaware (unknowing) *vs.* unawares (caught by surprise)

> We were *unaware* that you had already finished medical school.
> The security guard caught the thief *unawares*.

V

venal (capable of being bribed or corrupted) *vs.* venial (forgivable, pardonable)

A *venal* bookkeeper can do more harm to a company than can their chief competitors.

It was a *venial* offense; the supervisor decided not to enter it onto his permanent record.

vie *with*

Egotistical people *vie with* everyone else to be the center of attention.

vis-à-vis (face to face with, in comparison with)

W

who (*referring to a person*) *vs.* that (*referring to either a person or thing*) *vs.* which (*referring to a thing*)

The man *who* recognized you was my father.

The problem *that* prevents us from succeeding is primarily financial.

The book *which* the woman borrowed was never returned.

Challenges 47–52: Mastering Correct Usage

The following challenges test your knowledge on the Correct Usage Master List. For each multiple-choice question, circle the answer that best completes the sentence. Pay close attention to spelling, troublesome words, variations in meaning, verb/preposition parts, and synonyms.

Challenge 47

1. The bookkeeper _____
    the lawyer's request that she turn
    over the ledgers.
    a. receded to
    b. acceded to
    c. acceded
    d. acceded with

2. Even after three months of private
    lessons, she still did not have the
    _____ to speak any
    French.
    a. capacity
    b. ability
    c. celerity
    d. capaciousness

3. If you really want to _____
    significant changes, you must be
    willing to sacrifice personal time
    and pleasures.
    a. affect
    b. effect
    c. efect
    d. effact

4. She was always willing to
    _____ new employees
    about how to adjust to their new
    jobs.
    a. advocate
    b. advice
    c. adverse
    d. advise

5. The young princess was always
    _____ her chaperone
    when she traveled abroad.
    a. accompanied by
    b. accompanied
    c. accompanied with
    d. accompanied in

6. Even the poorest child can dream
    of _____ his greatest goal.
    a. chiefing
    b. acheiving
    c. achieveing
    d. achieving

7. They will be _____ their
    behavior, whether they accept the
    responsibility or not.
    a. accountable for
    b. accountable to
    c. accountable in
    d. accountable with

8. In _____ the regulations
    of the health department, the res-
    taurant required chest X-rays of
    all new employees.
    a. accord
    b. according
    c. accordance with
    d. accordance to

9. The doctor says you must
    _____ any alcohol for at
    least forty-eight hours after the
    operation.
    a. obtain
    b. abstain
    c. abstain from
    d. abstain against

10. She was _____ mention-
    ing her boss's private conversation
    without his permission.
    a. adverse to
    b. averse to
    c. advert to
    d. avert with

Challenge 48

1. After much coaxing, the belligerent child _____ cleaning his bedroom.
   a. asserted to
   b. asserted with
   c. averted to
   d. assented to

2. Wishing to reassure her unhappy child, the woman told him that everything would be _____.
   a. alright
   b. helpless
   c. hopeless
   d. all right

3. I was glad to see that the book made _____ to Dr. Rosado's years of assistance and encouragement.
   a. illusion
   b. allusion
   c. efferent
   d. reference

4. After listening to the monotonous lectures of the professor, even the most interested students were developing an _____ an otherwise interesting subject.
   a. apathy about
   b. apathy with
   c. apology to
   d. apathy toward

5. Many people who seem cold, holding themselves _____ their neighbors, are actually just very shy.
   a. aloof in
   b. aloof of
   c. aloof from
   d. aloof by

6. The bulk of the inheritance was distributed _____ the eight children.
   a. between
   b. through
   c. among
   d. for

7. The grieving father wanted nothing more than to _____ his daughter's tragic accident at the hands of a drunken driver.
   a. revenge
   b. justify
   c. categorize
   d. avenge

8. By placing mirrors along the hallway, he created the _____ of spaciousness.
   a. illusion
   b. delusion
   c. allusion
   d. collusion

9. After knocking over the school bully, Jennifer said, "Looks like your bubble just _____, bully!"
   a. bursted
   b. burst
   c. inflated
   d. busted

10. The child's whining _____ the passengers around him, especially late at night.
    a. irritated
    b. aggravated
    c. exacerbated
    d. arrogated

Challenge 49

1. In order to raise money quickly, the company decided to _____ itself _____ assets not important to its profits.
   a. divest . . . from
   b. diversify . . . into
   c. divest . . . of
   d. divest . . . with

2. Sometimes the only solution to a bitter dispute is to place the matter before _____ party for arbitration.
   a. an uninterested
   b. an unusual
   c. a disinterested
   d. a non-interested

3. Given the projected decrease of job opportunities in the media, the guidance counselor _____ the student _____ majoring in broadcasting.
   a. discouraged . . . from
   b. discouraged . . . about
   c. discouraged . . . against
   d. discouraged . . . to

4. Until the child agreed to _____ drawing pictures on the living room walls, he was not allowed to watch television.
   a. desist in
   b. desisted from
   c. desist from
   d. divest from

5. The coroner was unable to make a _____ statement about the cause of death until he established the _____ time of death.
   a. definitive . . . definite
   b. definative . . . definite
   c. definite . . . definitive
   d. defensive . . . defendant

6. The prosecutor pointed dramatically at the _____ before facing the jury and making his opening statement.
   a. defendent
   b. defendor
   c. defendant
   d. defensant

7. The Chief of Staff of the Army must be prepared to deal with _____ occurring simultaneously around the world.
   a. crisis
   b. criterion
   c. human drama
   d. crises

8. High school authorities will often refer a troublesome student to the guidance _____.
   a. chancellor
   b. counselor
   c. councilor
   d. consul

9. She slept fitfully that night, awaking _____.
   a. continuously
   b. consistently
   c. continually
   d. contentedly

10. Although such a mixture would make anyone nauseated, my brother likes to _____ vodka and root beer.
    a. drank
    b. drunk
    c. drink
    d. drinken

Challenge 50

1. The grains of sand on the beach were so _____ that they were barely distinguishable to the eye.
   a. minuscule
   b. miniscule
   c. minscule
   d. minascule

2. Although similar in many respects, television, radio, and cable TV are very different _____.
   a. mediums
   b. medium
   c. medias
   d. media

3. "Never _____ sight of all the _____ ends such a large project creates," the boss advised, "because they'll trip you up if you do."
   a. loose . . . lose
   b. loose . . . loose
   c. lose . . . lose
   d. lose . . . loose

4. Because all the students wore blue blazers and red ties, they were a_____ group in that respect.
   a. homogeneous
   b. homogenous
   c. homologous
   d. homogenized

5. The freshman was _____ the senior computer student for all the help she'd given him on his homework assignments.
   a. grateful to
   b. grateful for
   c. grateful because
   d. grateful toward

6. "We all know that the _____ acts in our best interest," the press secretary asserted.
   a. goverment
   b. governement
   c. govement
   d. government

7. She wanted to explore the woodlands her _____ had purchased centuries ago.
   a. forbears
   b. forebares
   c. forebears
   d. forbares

8. There are likely to be _____ students enrolling in law school now that the job market is so tight.
   a. fewer
   b. many
   c. less
   d. lesser

9. Only members who carried their membership cards were allowed to enter the reception; all others were _____ the festivities.
   a. excluded in
   b. excluded with
   c. excluded from
   d. excluded for

10. The new movie theater _____ the property value of the shopping district.
    a. enhanced
    b. enlightened
    c. asserted
    d. improved

Challenge 51

1. The disease _____ spread throughout the island decimated the population.
   a. which
   b. who
   c. that
   d. then

2. When a liquid is dense, dark, or thick with matter, it can be said to be _____.
   a. turgid
   b. turbid
   c. turbine
   d. turbent

3. A trail filled with twists, turns, and winding sections is _____.
   a. tortuous
   b. torturous
   c. tortured
   d. torsion

4. It is far easier for a sharpshooter to hit a _____ target than a moving one.
   a. statue
   b. stationary
   c. stationery
   d. standstill

5. "_____ the moment" is the motto of people who don't want to waste any opportunity in life.
   a. sieze
   b. seize
   c. seige
   d. siege

6. Many people are attracted to music because of its _____.
   a. rhythem
   b. rythm
   c. rhythm
   d. rhythym

7. The spirited horse had to be _____ in by the rider.
   a. reigned
   b. rained
   c. reined
   d. riegned

8. A church's body of laws is known as a _____.
   a. cannon
   b. canon
   c. tenet
   d. canen

9. An alliance of political parties is called a _____.
   a. block
   b. blockard
   c. blockade
   d. bloc

10. Shuttlecocks in _____ are the equivalent of tennis balls in tennis.
    a. badmitten
    b. badminten
    c. badmitton
    d. badminton

Challenge 52

1. After their store went out of business, the entire family was in terrible _____.
   a. straights
   b. straits
   c. streits
   d. strates

2. "I knew I _____ studied harder," the girl moaned after receiving a poor grade on the test.
   a. should of
   b. should
   c. should have
   d. shall

3. The fresh peaches, velvety and aromatic, were a _____ delight.
   a. sensuous
   b. sensual
   c. sensitive
   d. sentient

4. After watching seven football games in a row, James was _____ television.
   a. satiated from
   b. satiated by
   c. satiated with
   d. satiated in

5. Although the little boy had anticipated Hallowe'en happily, he ran away whenever he _____ a doorbell, convinced a goblin would emerge.
   a. rang
   b. had rung
   c. had rang
   d. runged

6. The writer _____ the attention he received after winning the great Pulitzer Prize for his novel.
   a. revelled in
   b. revelled from
   c. revelled with
   d. revelled

7. Driving a car while under the influence of alcohol is _____ loss of license, imprisonment, and fines.
   a. punishable with
   b. punishable by
   c. punishable in
   d. punishable through

8. If one is not discreet, it is very easy to gain _____ in a small town.
   a. negativity
   b. notoriety
   c. notoriousness
   d. negativism

9. Unusual or unaccountable occurrences are called _____.
   a. phenomenons
   b. phenomeni
   c. phenomenuns
   d. phenomena

10. The couple enjoyed a happy marriage because they _____ tolerating and understanding each other's little quirks.
    a. persevered about
    b. persevered into
    c. persevered in
    d. preserved in

Challenge 53: Problem Pairs

Using your understanding of the Correct Usage Master List, select the correct word to complete each sentence.

1. tortuous/torturous

    It was a _____ journey for the injured man as the Jeep bounced and rumbled along the _____ mountain path.

2. reluctant/reticent

    I am _____ to go to a party with a blind date as _____ as your friend.

3. discrete/discreet

    Please be more _____ about your opinions around here; it would be better to keep your personal life and your professional life _____.

4. stationary/stationery

    Because of the traffic jam, the _____ store's truck was _____ at the corner.

5. loathe/loath

    I _____ poached fish, but I am _____ to tell the hostess.

6. incredible/incredulous

    We were totally _____ when he gave such an _____ excuse.

7. irritate/aggravate

Do not _____ a bad situation by continuing to _____ your neighbors with such loud music.

8. (past tense of lie/past tense of lay)

After I _____ the tiles in the bathroom yesterday, I _____ down for a nap.

Problems with Verb Forms

The following irregular (or *strong*) verb forms frequently confuse people. As their forms change without a predictable pattern, you would do well to remember them.

Present	Past	Past Participle
awake	awoke	(have) awoken
bid	bade	(have) bidden
bite	bit	(have) bitten
blow	blew	(have) blown
break	broke	(have) broken
cleave	cleft	(have) cloven
dive	dove	(have) dived
draw	drew	(have) drawn
fly	flew	(have) flown
forsake	forsook	(have) forsaken
lay	laid	(have) laid
leave	left	(have) left
lie	lay	(have) lain
melt	melted	(have) molten
mow	mowed	(have) mown
rise	rose	(have) risen
shave	shaved	(have) shaven
show	showed	(have) shown
slay	slew	(have) slain
strike	struck	(have) stricken
swear	swore	(have) sworn
tear	tore	(have) torn
tread	trod	(have) trodden

Challenge 54: Verb Forms

Fill in the correct forms of the following verbs, supplying the present tense, past tense, or past participle for each word given.

Present	Past	Past Participle
_____	awoke	_____
bid	_____	_____
_____	_____	have bound
_____	bit	_____
blow	_____	_____
_____	_____	have broken
_____	cleft	_____
dive	_____	_____
_____	_____	have drawn
fly	_____	_____
_____	forsook	_____
_____	_____	have laid
_____	left	_____
_____	_____	have lain
melt	_____	_____
_____	_____	have mown
_____	rose	_____
_____	_____	have shaven
slay	_____	_____
_____	struck	_____

		have sworn
_____	swelled	_____
tear	_____	_____
_____	_____	have trodden

Problems with Plurals

When forming the plural of a compound word, always remember that you add the "s" to the most significant noun. For example, when forming the plural of "daughter-in-law," *daughter* is the most significant noun, not *law*; so the correct plural form would be *daughters-in-law*, not *daughter-in-laws*.

Challenge 55: Compound Plurals

Try your hand at giving the correct plural form for each of these compounds words.

1. mother-in-law
2. sargeant-at-arms
3. man-of-war
4. court-martial
5. chief-of-staff
6. right-of-way
7. attorney-general
8. aide-de-camp
9. vice-president
10. son-in-law

In English, almost all nouns form the plural by adding "s" (*boy, boys*). But there are several groups of nouns that don't quite follow that rule or the other rules implied by it. For example, there are words that have no singular form, yet have a plural (*pants*). Others that have no plural form often have a singular (*music*). There's another group called collective nouns (*jury*) which imply a plural, more than one, yet take a singular verb.

Challenge 56: Irregular Plurals

The following words do not conform to regular rules for creating plurals. Assign each word to one of these categories: Irregular Plurals, Collective Nouns, Nouns with no Singular, Nouns with no Plural.

committee	trousers	scissors	deer	army
child	louse	courage	crowd	brother
cattle	class	goose	billiards	sheep
wheat	team	crew	shears	pliers

Irregular Plurals (give plural form, too)

_____

_____

Collective Nouns

_____

_____

Nouns with no Singular

_____

_____

Nouns with no Plural

_____

_____

Problems with Pronunciation

Here's an exercise that will help you to understand the importance of using your dictionary. After each of these problem words, the phonetic spelling is included as it would appear in a dictionary entry. Most of the phonetic spellings are easy to understand—the only unusual symbol, the *schwa* (ə), is roughly pronounced like an unaccented *uh* or *eh*. Next time you come across a new word in your reading, try to learn how the word is pronounced as well as what it means.

aborigine	ăb-ə-rĭj'-ə-nē	**lascivious**	lə-sĭv'-ē-əs
acetic	ə-sē'-tĭk	**liaison**	lē'-ə-zon
apropos	ăp-rə-pō'	**lien**	lēn
baroque	bə-rōk'	**machination**	māk-ĭ-nā'-shən
bayou	bī'-ōō	**mien**	mēn
brooch	brōch	**niche**	nĭch
buoy	bōō'-ē	**nonpareil**	nŏn-pə-rĕl'
cello	chĕl'-ō	**nuance**	nōō-ans'
chamois	shăm'-ē	**oblique**	ō-blēk'
chic	shēk	**onerous**	ŏn'-ər-əs
corps	kōr	**parfait**	par-fā'
coup	kōō	**philistine**	fĭl-ĭs'-tēn
debris	də-brē'	**phebian**	plĭ-bē'-an
discern	dĭ-surn'	**poignant**	poin'-yənt
facade	fə-sahd'	**posthumous**	pŏs'-chōō-məs
fuselage	fyōō'-sə-lahzh	**puerile**	pwĕr'-īl
guerilla	gə-rĭl'-ə	**regime**	rā-zhēm'
harbinger	hahr'-bən-jər	**renege**	rĭ-nĕg'
heifer	hĕf'-ər	**reveille**	rĕv'-ə-lē
heinous	hā'-nəs	**rudiment**	rōō'-də-mənt
hosiery	hō'-zhə-rē	**specious**	spē'-shəs
imbroglio	ĭm-brōl'-yō	**subpoena**	sə-pē'-nə
inchoate	ĭn-kō'-ĭt	**thyme**	tīm
irascible	ĭ-răs'-ə-bəl	**travail**	tra-vāl'
isthmus	ĭs'-məs	**usury**	yōō'-zhə-rē

Problems with Spelling

The English language can be one of the most difficult to master—ask anyone who's tried to figure out the spelling rules. Here are twelve of the most commonly misspelled words, along with some tricks to help you remember the correct spelling.

	Wrong	**Right**	**Remember!**
1.	acheive	achieve	*I* Excel
2.	defendent	defendant	He *anti*cipates a verdict.
3.	embarasment	embarrassment	*Really Red for Silly Statement*
4.	enviroment	environment	There's *iron* in the environment.
5.	goverment	government	The *govern*or *govern*s the government.
6.	hygeine	hygiene	Cleanliness *Is Essential.*
7.	judgement	judgment	Only the *E*nglish add E.
8.	liason	liaison	A Liaison *Is Always Important.*
9.	miniscule	minuscule	There's *minus* in minuscule.
10.	sacreligious	sacrilegious	Sacrilegious acts are not *religious*.
11.	seperate	separate	Se*para*te the *part*s.
12.	temperment	temperament	There's *a temper* in temperament.

Challenge 57: Spelling Problems

Can you identify which of the following words are spelled correctly? If you find one that's not, see if you can provide the correct spelling.

1. goverment   1. _____

2. liaison   2. _____

3. guerila   3. _____

4. miniscule   4. _____

5. judgement   5. _____

6. chamis   6. _____

7. sacrilegious   7. _____

8. separate   8. _____

9. phillistine   9. _____

10. lascivious   10. _____

Challenge 58: *-Sede, -Ceed,* or *-Cede?*

This potential spelling problem is easily cured: only one word in English ends with -sede (supersede), three words with -ceed (exceed, proceed, succeed) and all others end with -cede. With that in mind, choose the correct spelling of the following words.

1. supercede / supersede   1. _____

2. intersede / intercede   2. _____

3. accede / acceed   3. _____

4. exceed / excede   4. _____

5. resede / recede   5. _____

6. concede / consede   6. _____

7. proceed / prosede   7. _____

8. seceed / secede   8. _____

9. precede / presede   9. _____

10. succeed / succede   10. _____

Challenge 59: *-Able* or *-Ible?*

Should that word you just wrote end with *-able* or *-ible?* It's actually easy to figure out, especially when you realize that four out of five words ending with that 'sound' will end with *-able,* and that all new words coined to end with that sound will end with *-able.* The clue to figuring it out: if the abstract noun form ends with *-ation,* the adjective will end with *-able;* if the abstract noun form ends with *-ition, -tion, -sion,* or *-ion,* the adjective will end with *-ible.* Try your hand at these.

Verb	Noun	Adjective
1. admire	_____	_____
2. admit	_____	_____
3. exhaust	_____	_____
4. inflame	_____	_____
5. convert	_____	_____
6. imagine	_____	_____
7. immerse	_____	_____
8. permit	_____	_____
9. adore	_____	_____
10. comprehend	_____	_____

Part IV

A MASTERFUL VOCABULARY

1000 Essential Words

Module 1: Abase—Cerebral

Group 1

abase   to humble or humiliate.
The French Revolution *abased* the proud nobility.

abate   to make less in amount, degree, force.
The tempest *abates* in fury.

abbreviate   to make shorter.
When he saw that the meeting was running late, he *abbreviated* his comments.

abdicate   to give up formally a high office, throne, or authority.
The father *abdicated* his responsibility by not setting a good example for the boy.

aberration   a departure from what is right, true, or correct.
Many hospital patients suffer from mental *aberrations*.

abet   to incite, sanction, or help in wrongdoing.
Aiding and *abetting* an enemy of the country constitutes treason.

abeyance   temporary suspension, as of an activity or function.
The strike motion was held in *abeyance* pending contract negotiations.

abhor   to shrink from in fear, disgust, or hatred; detest.
The pacifist *abhors* war.

abide by   to submit to, put up with.
We will *abide by* the decision of the court.

ability   a being able; power to do something.
Her scores clearly indicated a remarkable *ability* for calculus.

abject   of the lowest degree; miserable; wretched.
Many Asians live in a state of *abject* poverty.

abjure   to give up (rights, allegiance, etc.) on oath; renounce.
A new citizen must *abjure* allegiance to his former country.

ablution   a washing of the body, esp. as a religious ceremony.
Ablutions are a part of many religious rites.

abnegate   to deny and refuse; give up (rights, claims, etc.); renounce.
He must *abnegate* all his former friends.

abolish   to do away with, as an institution.
Slavery was *abolished* in Massachusetts shortly after the American Revolution.

abominate   to have feelings of hatred and disgust for; loathe.
I *abominate* all laws that deprive people of their rights.

abortive   coming to nothing; unsuccessful; fruitless.
The rebels made an *abortive* attempt to capture the radio station.

abrade   to scrape or rub off; wear away by scraping or rubbing.
Sandpaper is used to *abrade* a rough surface.

abrasive   scraping or rubbing, annoyingly harsh or jarring.
The high-pitched whine of the machinery was *abrasive* to my nerves.

abridge   to reduce in scope or extent; shorten.
The paperback book was an *abridged* edition.

abrogate   to cancel or appeal by authority; annul.
Congress has the right to *abrogate* laws with the consent of the chief executive.

abscond   to go away hastily and secretly; run away and hide, esp. in order to escape the law.
The teller *absconded* with the bank's funds.

absolution   a formal freeing from guilt or obligation; forgiveness.
The clergy has the right to grant *absolution*.

abstain   to hold oneself back; voluntarily do without; refrain.
Alcoholics must *abstain* from any indulgence in alcoholic drinks.

abstemious   moderate, esp. in eating and drinking.

> The *abstemious* eater is seldom overweight.

Group 2

abstruse   hard to understand; recondite; deep.

> The concepts of Albert Einstein were *abstruse* even to physicists.

abut   to join end to end.

> When estates *abut*, borders must be defined properly.

accede   to enter upon the duties of an office; attain to.

> He *acceded* to their request.

accelerate   to increase in speed.

> Going downhill, a vehicle will naturally *accelerate*.

accept   to take what is offered or given; receive, esp. willingly.

> They *accepted* their responsibility to meet the deadline.

access   the act of coming toward or near to; approach.

> Public libraries insure that people have *access* to vast stores of information.

acclaim   to greet with loud approval; applaud.

> The crowd in the square *acclaimed* their hero as the new president.

acclimate   to accustom to a new environment.

> Visitors to the desert have a hard time *acclimating* themselves to the extreme variations in temperature.

acclivity   an upward slope of ground.

> He viewed the great *acclivity* with dismay as their car chugged along.

accumulate   to gather over a period of time; to pile up.

> Over the years she has *accumulated* a large collection of antique bric-a-brac.

accustom   to make familiar by custom.

> The supervisor was not *accustomed* to having her instructions ignored.

acerbity   a sour, astringent quality.

> The *acerbity* of her wit won her many enemies.

acoustic   pertaining to hearing or with sound.
　　The *acoustic* qualities of a room may be improved by insulation.

acquiesce   to agree or consent quietly without protest, but without enthusiasm.
　　One must often *acquiesce* to the demands of a superior.

acquit   to release from a duty or obligation.
　　The jury *acquitted* the defendant.

acrimony   bitterness or harshness of temper, manner, or speech; asperity.
　　His *acrimony* resulted from years of disappointment.

actuate   to put into action or motion.
　　The machine was *actuated* by an electric starter.

acumen   keenness and quickness in understanding and dealing with a situation; shrewdness.
　　The *acumen* of many early industrialists accounts for their success.

adamant   inflexible; hard.
　　A man must be *adamant* in his determination to succeed.

adaptable   able to adjust or be made suitable to new circumstances.
　　Thanks to the intelligence that has made technology possible, humans are more *adaptable* to a variety of climates than any other species.

adduce   bring forward as a reason or example.
　　In their defense they *adduced* several justifications for their actions.

adept   highly skilled; expert.
　　A journalist is *adept* at the use of words.

adequate   sufficient; good enough for what is required or needed.
　　Without *adequate* sunlight, many tropical plants will not bloom.

adhere   to stick fast; stay attached.
　　Many persons *adhere* to their beliefs despite all arguments.

adjourn   to close a session or meeting for a time.
　　Since it is now five o'clock, I move that we *adjourn* until tomorrow morning.

Group 3

adjunct   a thing added to something else, but secondary or not essential to it.
A rider is an *adjunct* to a legislative bill.

adjure   to charge or command solemnly, often under oath or penalty.
The witness was *adjured* to weigh his words carefully.

admonish   to warn; to caution against specific faults.
The child was *admonished* not to run into the roadway.

adroit   skillful in a physical or mental way; clever; expert.
The *adroit* juggler held the attention of the crowd.

adulation   to praise too highly; flattery.
The *adulation* tendered to the wealthy is often aimed at their purses.

adumbration   to obscure or overshadow.
The first atomic bomb was an *adumbration* of a new era of destruction.

advent   coming, arrival.
The *advent* of spring is always a gay time.

adventitious   added from outside; not inherent; accidental.
The *adventitious* economic aid given by the United States was instrumental
in saving many nations from Communism.

adverse   opposing; moving or working in an opposite direction.
Adverse winds are a hazard to sailing craft.

adversity   misfortune; poverty; a state of wretchedness.
Shakespeare praised the "sweet uses" of *adversity*.

advocate   to plead or urge for another's cause.
Socialists *advocate* public ownership of utilities.

aesthetic   pertaining to the beautiful; sensitive to art and beauty; showing good
taste; artistic.
Modern design seeks to produce machines which have *aesthetic* as well as
functional appeal. Also: esthetic.

affable   plesant, and easy to talk to or approach; friendly.
The smiling face and *affable* manner of the agent put the child at ease.

affect   to influence.

The judge did not allow his personal feelings to *affect* his judgment of the case's legal merits.

affiliation   connection, as with an organization.

His *affiliation* with the club has been of long standing; he has been a member for over ten years.

affinity   relationship; kinship.

There is a close *affinity* among many European languages.

affirmation   solemn avowal; positive declaration; assertion.

Quakers and others may testify in court on *affirmation*.

affix   to attach, fasten.

A price tag was *affixed* to each item.

affluent   plentiful; abundant.

The United States is an *affluent* nation.

agglomerate   to form into a ball; to gather into one mass.

It was necessary to *agglomerate* all the minerals into one product to produce the necessary weight.

aggravate   to make worse; make more burdensome, troublesome.

His sarcasm only *aggravated* an already touchy situation.

aggregate   gathered into or considered as a whole; total.

The *aggregate* of uranium ores in the Colorado plateau amazed prospectors.

aggression   unprovoked attack or warlike act.

The invasion of Afghanistan was denounced in the Western press as *aggression*.

agitate   to sir up or shake up; to move violently.

Rumors of change in the government *agitated* the population.

agnostic   one who does not think it possible to know whether or not God exists.

Many *agnostics* are converted to religion in their later years.

Group 4

alacrity   liveliness; briskness.

The *alacrity* shown by the new employee gratified the manager.

alibi   a defensive excuse.

> His *alibi* was ironclad; he was in the hospital at the time of the murder.

alienate   to make unfriendly; estrange.

> One purpose of the offer to the East was to *alienate* the Western nations.

allay   to put fears to rest; to pacify, calm.

> Therapy will often *allay* the fears of the neurotic.

alleviate   to make less hard to bear; lighten or relieve pain, suffering.

> The morphine helped to *alleviate* the pain.

allocate   to distribute in shares or according to a plan; allot.

> The new serum was *allocated* among the states by population.

allude   to refer indirectly or casually or by suggestion.

> The report *alludes* to a later document.

aloof   at a distance; removed.

> Her elegant appearance and formal politeness made her seem *aloof*, though in reality she was only shy.

altercation   an angry or heated argument.

> The *altercation* stopped just short of physical violence.

altitude   height, especially above sea level or the earth's surface.

> The plane had reached an *altitude* of four miles.

altruism   unselfish concern for the welfare of others; selflessness.

> The *altruism* of the nursing profession is taken for granted.

amalgamate   to join together into one; unite; combine.

> We will have to *amalgamate* all our groups in order to be strong.

amass   to pile up; collect together.

> Through careful investment he had *amassed* a sizable fortune.

ambidextrous   able to use both hands with equal ease.

> *Ambidextrous* tennis players have a great advantage.

ambiguous   having two or more possible meanings.

> The *ambiguous* nature of many legislative acts requires clarification by the courts.

ambivalent   simultaneous conflicting feelings toward a person or thing.

I am *ambivalent* about the job; although the atmosphere is pleasant, the work itself is boring.

ambulatory   of or for walking.

Ambulatory patients require organized activities to speed their recovery.

ameliorate   make or become better; improve.

It will take more than a few new textbooks to *ameliorate* the crisis in the schools.

amenable   able to be controlled or influenced; responsible; submissive.

He was *amenable* to any proposition.

amicable   friendly in feelings; showing good will; peaceable.

Courts often seek to settle civil suits in an *amicable* manner.

amnesty   a general pardon, esp. for political offenses against a government.

The president granted *amnesty* to the rebels.

amoral   without moral sense or principles; incapable of distinguishing between right and wrong.

To the new settlers, the islanders seemed to lead a carefree, *amoral* existence, doing whatever they pleased.

amplify   to make larger or stronger; increase or extend power, authority.

Congressmen may *amplify* their remarks for appearance in the Record.

anachronism   anything that is or seems out of its proper time in history.

An abstract picture in an early American home is an *anachronism*.

analogy   a similarity in some respects between things otherwise unlike; partial likeness.

Countless poets have pointed out the *analogy* between youth and springtime.

Group 5

anarchy   complete absence of government.

When the police union strikes, *anarchy* may soon follow.

animosity   a feeling of strong dislike or hatred; ill will.

The *animosity* of the population of the occupied territories made the value of its labor doubtful to the conqueror.

annals   a written account of events year by year; chronological records.
> The *annals* of the scientific societies reflect the advance of our era.

annihilate   to destroy completely; to put out of existence; demolish.
> If the government does not act to preserve the few remaining herds, the whole species will have been *annihilated* by the end of the century.

annotation   a critical or explanatory note.
> *Annotations* are sometimes the most interesting part of a text, but they are often overlooked.

annual   of or measured by a year.
> The company holds an *annual* picnic on the Fourth of July.

annuity   a payment of a fixed sum of money at regular intervals of time, esp. yearly.
> Investment in an *annuity* provides an income for one's old age.

annul   to do away with; put an end to.
> The Supreme Court can *annul* a law which is unconstitutional.

anomalous   deviating from the regular arrangement, general rule, or usual method; abnormal.
> An *anomalous* jukebox stood rusting in the square of the primitive village.

anonymous   with no name known or acknowledged.
> Little credence should be given to an *anonymous* accusation.

antecedent   any happening or thing prior to another.
> All history is a repetition of *antecedents*.

anterior   coming before in time, order, or logic; previous; earlier.
> The *anterior* section of the boy's brain was damaged in the accident.

antipathetic   opposed or antagonistic in character, tendency.
> Siblings are often *antipathetic*.

antipathy   a strong or deep-rooted dislike; aversion.
> She had an *antipathy* toward men.

antithesis   a contrast or opposition of thoughts.
> Black is the *antithesis* of white.

apathetic   feeling little or no emotion; unmoved.
> The *apathetic* attitude of voters enables a minority to control the election.

aperture   opening; hole; gap.

> The woman walked through an *aperture* between two rocks and found herself in a cave.

aplomb   self-possession; assurance; poise.

> His *aplomb* is characteristic of the successful urbanite.

appease   to pacify or quiet, esp. by giving in to the demands of.

> Only a heartfelt apology will *appease* his rage at having been slighted.

append   to attach; affix; add as a supplement or appendix.

> Exhibits should be *appended* to the report.

apposite   suited to the purpose; appropriate; apt.

> Since he hadn't followed the discussion, his comments were not *apposite*.

apprehensive   anxious or fearful about the future; uneasy.

> She was *apprehensive* about the examination.

apprise   to inform or notify.

> He was captured because none could *apprise* him of the enemy advance.

approbation   official approval, sanction or commendation.

> The act was performed with the *approbation* of his superiors.

arbitrary   based on one's preference, notion, or whim; capricious.

> An *arbitrary* ruling of a civil commission may be reviewed by the courts.

Group 6

archaic   that has ceased to be used except for special purposes, as in poetry or church ritual.

> Some words like "thou" are *archaic*.

archetype   the original pattern or model from which all other things of the same kind are made; prototype.

> Solomon is the *archetype* of the wise man.

archives   a place where public records or documents are kept.

> A separate building houses the United States *archives* in Washington.

arrogate   to claim or seize without right; appropriate to oneself arrogantly.

> He *arrogates* to himself the judicial power.

artifice   trickery or craft.

He used every *artifice* to win the contract.

ascertain   to find out with certainty.

Because the woman's story was so confused, we have been unable to *ascertain* whether a crime was committed or not.

ascetic   a person who leads a life of contemplation and rigorous self-denial.

As an *ascetic,* he ate only the simplest foods and never touched alcohol.

ascribe   to attribute, impute, or assign as a cause.

His death was *ascribed* to poison.

asperity   harshness or roughness.

The *asperity* of his decisions made the judge no friends.

aspersion   a damaging or disparaging remark; slander; innuendo.

Every pioneer in science has had *aspersions* cast on his work.

assert   to claim or state positively; declare; affirm.

He *asserted* his title to the property.

assumption   something taken for granted; supposition.

I prepared dinner on the *assumption* that they would be home by seven.

assure   to make a person sure of something; convince.

The fact that they left their tickets *assures* that they will return.

astral   of, from, or like the stars.

The number of *astral* bodies is beyond computation.

attenuate   make thin; dilute; weaken.

His mumbling delivery and hesitant manner *attenuated* the force of his remarks.

atypical   not typical; not characteristic; abnormal.

The usually calm man's burst of temper was *atypical.*

augment   to increase.

He *augments* his wealth with every deal.

aural   of or received through the ear or the sense of hearing.

Since the sound system was not working properly, the *aural* aspect of the performance was a disappointment.

auspicious   favored by fortune; successful.

    The first week's business was an *auspicious* start for the whole enterprise.

autocrat   a domineering, self-willed person.

    The *autocratic* attitude of the Russian ruling class elicited resentment from the people.

averse   not willing or inclined; reluctant; opposed to.

    The perennial bachelor is *averse* to matrimony.

avert   to keep from happening; ward off.

    By acting quickly we *averted* the disaster.

avocation   hobby; something one does in addition to his vocation or regular work, and usually for pleasure.

    The person who can earn a living from his *avocation* is indeed fortunate.

baleful   harmful or threatening harm or evil; ominous; deadly.

    The *baleful* glance of a witch was feared.

banal   commonplace; trite.

    The use of *banal* remarks will dull any conversation.

Group 7

baneful   causing distress, death, or ruin; deadly.

    The ex-convict exerted a *baneful* influence on the other members of the group.

bastion   a projection from a fortification, arranged to give a wider firing range.

    The *bastion* projects outward from the main enclosure.

beguile   to mislead by cheating or tricking; deceive.

    Where he found himself weak, he would *beguile* the opposition into applauding his propositions.

belabor   to beat severely; hit or whip.

    In the book, the poor servant was constantly *belabored* without cause.

belie   to tell lies about.

    Her laughing face *belied* her pretense of annoyance.

belittle   to make seem little, less important; speak slightingly of; deprecate.

    He *belittled* the actress's talent by suggesting that her beauty, rather than her acting ability, was responsible for her success.

bellicose of a quarrelsome or hostile nature; eager to fight or quarrel; warlike.

The *bellicose* attitude of the man involved him in many fights.

benediction a blessing.

Many sought the *benediction* of their pastor during troubled times.

beneficiary any one receiving benefit or inheritance.

The man named his wife as the *beneficiary* of the insurance policy.

benign good-natured; kindly.

His *benign* influence helped to alleviate the suffering of the poor.

berate to scold or rebuke severely.

The teacher who *berates* his class is rationalizing his own faults.

bibliography list of sources of information on a given subject or period.

She assembled a *bibliography* of major works on American history published since 1960.

biennial happening every two years.

Many state legislatures convene on a *biennial* basis.

biped a two-footed animal.

Man and birds are listed among the *bipeds.*

blatant disagreeably loud or boisterous; offensively noisy; clamorous.

The herds of cattle filled the air with their *blatant* bellowing.

blithe showing a gay, cheerful disposition; carefree.

Her *blithe* spirit provided an air of gaiety to the whole event.

bombastic using or characterized by high-sounding but unimportant or meaningless language; grandiloquent; pompous.

The *bombastic* politician sounds like a fool on television.

breach opening or gap; failure to keep the terms, as of a promise or law.

When they failed to deliver the goods, they were guilty of a *breach* of contract.

brevity conciseness, terseness.

Brevity is the essence of journalistic writing.

bucolic pertaining to a farm, country life; rural.

The *bucolic* personality is usually thought of as hearty, simple, and lusty.

burgeon   to sprout; to put forth buds, shoots, etc.

   Plants *burgeon* with the coming of spring.

burnish   to make or become shiny; polish by rubbing.

   Burnished metal will gleam in the light.

cadence   rhythmic flow, modulation of speech, measured movement.

   The low and musical *cadence* of her voice was a delight to hear.

cadre   basic structure or framework.

   A *cadre* of commissioned and non-commissioned officers was maintained.

calligraphy   beautiful handwriting, esp. as an art.

   The *calligraphy* of the monks is the basis of many printing typefaces today.

Group 8

callow   immature; young and inexperienced.

   A *callow* youth often grows into a sophisticated man.

calumniate   to slander; to spread false and harmful statements about.

   He was known to *caluminiate* anyone who disagreed with him.

calumny   trickery, slander, accusation.

   Many honest persons are the victims of *calumny*.

candor   the quality of being fair and unprejudiced; impartiality.

   Candor and innocence often go hand-in-hand.

capacious   able to contain or hold much; roomy; spacious.

   The *capacious* railroad terminals offer a bright welcome to tourists.

capacity   ability or aptitude.

   His prudent decisions proved his *capacity* for the top job.

capital   most significant; of or having to do with capital or wealth.

   That was a *capital* idea!
   An outlay of *capital* is necessary when starting a business.

capitol   a legislative building, such as the building in which the U.S. Congress meets at Washington, D.C.

   The state Senate convened in the *capitol* today.

capitulate   to give up on prearranged condition; surrender conditionally.

   The city *capitulated* to the victors.

capricious   changing suddenly; willfully erratic; flighty.

   The lady is *capricious*; today she likes me, tomorrow she likes someone else.

captious fond of catching others in mistakes; fault-finding; quibbling; carping.

His *captious* criticisms were motivated by an unreasoning jealousy.

careen tip to one side.

The ship *careened* with each new wave.

carnage bloody and extensive slaughter, esp. in battle; massacre; bloodshed.

The *carnage* of modern warfare is frightful to consider.

carnal in or of the body or flesh; material or worldly; not spiritual.

The *carnal* pleasures of Babylon were deplored by the ancients.

carnivorous flesh-eating.

Tigers are among the *carnivorous* animals.

castigate to punish or rebuke severely, esp. by harsh public criticism.

The judge *castigated* the plaintiff before he fined him for contempt of court.

casuistry application or misapplication of general ethical principles to specific cases.

His question, "If a man and wife are legally one, why must we buy two tickets?" was mere *casuistry*.

cataclysm any great upheaval that causes sudden, violent change, as an earthquake, war, etc.

Pompeii was visited by a *cataclysm* that destroyed the entire city.

catalyst substance that causes change in other substances without itself being affected.

Platinum is a *catalyst* in many processes; it speeds chemical changes without being affected itself.

caustic biting; burning; stinging.

The surface of the wood had been marred by some *caustic* substance.

cede to transfer the title of ownership of something.

A bill of sale will *cede* title of the property.

celerity swiftness in acting or moving; speed.

Act with all *celerity* to take advantage of the opportunity.

celestial heavenly; divine.

Planets are *celestial* bodies.

censure a judgment or resolution condemning a person for misconduct.

An act of *censure* may be enacted by the Senate.

cerebral pertaining to the brain or cerebrum.

The stroke was the result of a *cerebral* hemorrhage.

Challenge 60

Circle the word or phrase that will best complete the meaning of the sentence as a whole.

1. Because the mayor finished the speech in less than three minutes, those present applauded his _____.
   a. brevity
   b. sense of metaphor
   c. allusions
   d. timeliness
   e. sense of humor

2. _____ cannot exist within a democracy, which is a structured form of government.
   a. Anarchy
   b. Repression
   c. Socialism
   d. Education
   e. Liberalism

3. Unfortunately these favorable influences will _____ or even disappear within the next few years.
   a. defray
   b. recur
   c. abate
   d. vanish
   e. multiply

4. To give in to the terrorists' demands would be a betrayal of our responsibilities; such _____ would only encourage others to adopt similar methods for gaining their ends.
   a. defeats
   b. appeasement
   c. appeals
   d. subterfuge
   e. confusion

5. He was the chief _____ of his uncle's will. After taxes he was left with an inheritance worth close to twenty thousand dollars.
   a. exemption
   b. pensioner
   c. beneficiary
   d. contestant
   e. executor

6. His remarks were so _____ that we could not decide which of the possible meanings was correct.
   a. ambiguous
   b. facetious
   c. impalpable
   d. congruent
   e. specious

7. Scattered around the dead dragon were mementos of the _____: heads, arms, and torsos of young maidens.
   a. battle
   b. relics
   c. prom
   d. carnage
   e. festivities

8. Because the custom posed a danger to the children, the leaders of the community decided to _____ it.
   a. implement
   b. abolish
   c. fulfill
   d. continue
   e. determine

9. Because they offer a diversion from the more serious aspects of everyday life, stamp and coin collecting are _____.
   a. avocations
   b. adulterous
   c. adventurous
   d. enlightening
   e. expensive

10. She was _____ in her determination to achieve her goals.
    a. sweet
    b. adamant
    c. amoral
    d. helpful
    e. alluring

11. A(n) _____ assistant is a great help to any employer.
    a. sleepy
    b. adept
    c. absent
    d. left-handed
    e. angry

12. The woman, a lover of sweets, disliked the taste of the dill pickles because of their _____.
    a. dourness
    b. celerity
    c. celibacy
    d. acerbity
    e. juiciness

13. The Watergate scandal was the ostensible cause of Nixon's decision to _____ the presidency.
    a. abandon
    b. abdicate
    c. aspire to
    d. abort
    e. abridge

14. Although the Delphic Oracle warned Agamemnon of storms in the Mediterranean, he did not heed its _____, and his fleet was destroyed.
    a. admission
    b. admonition
    c. knowledge
    d. suggestion
    e. decision

15. Some historians contend that Hitler was a tyrant, unlike Franklin Roosevelt, who might have been considered an _____ ruler.
    a. egotistic
    b. absorbed
    c. alliterate
    d. absurd
    e. altruistic

Module 2: Chastisement–Elusive

Group 1

chastisement to scold or condemn sharply.

Chastisement of delinquent children is considered necessary by some teachers.

chide to scold or reprove mildly.

Parents should *chide* a disobedient child.

chronic long-lasting, recurring.

His *chronic* asthma flares up at certain times of the year.

chronology arrangement by time, list of events by order of occurence.

The book included a *chronology* of the poet's life against the background of the major political events of his age.

circuitous roundabout; indirect; devious.

Sometimes a *circuitous* route is the fastest way to reach your destination.

circumlocution a roundabout, indirect, or lengthy way of expressing something; periphrasis.

The audience was restive as the speaker's *circumlocution* went on and on without making a point.

circumspect careful to consider all related circumstances before acting, judging, or deciding; cautious, careful.

A public official must be *circumspect* in all his actions.

circumvent to get the better of or prevent from happening by craft or ingenuity.

By devious dealings, they were able to *circumvent* the regulations.

citation summons to appear in court; an official praise, as for bravery; reference to legal precedent or authority.

Caught for speeding, I received a *citation*.
Three firefighters received *citations* for the heroic rescue effort.
The attorney asked the clerk to check the *citations* to cases in the Supreme Court.

cite to quote.

The lawyer *cited* a previous decision to support his point.

clairvoyance the supposed ability to perceive things that are not in sight or that cannot be seen.

It was believed that the oracles had the power of *clairvoyance*.

cleave   this word has two opposite meanings:
(1) to adhere. Let us *cleave* together.
(2) to sever. The blow *cleaved* the limb in two.

clemency   forebearance, leniency, or mercy, as toward an offender or enemy.
The governor granted *clemency* to the prisoners.

coalesce   to grow together, as the halves of a broken bone.
The *coalescence* of the American states is one of the secrets of our nation's progress.

coalition   a combination; union.
Various environmentalist groups formed a *coalition* to work for the candidate most sympathetic to their cause.

coerce   to force or compel.
A false confession was *coerced* from him.

cogent   forceful and to the point, as a reason or argument; compelling; convincing.
A debater must present *cogent* arguments to win his point.

cogitate   to think seriously and deeply about; ponder; meditate; consider.
Take time to *cogitate* before you answer.

cognition   perception; process of knowing.
The mere *cognition* of a problem is only the first step toward a solution.

cognizant   having knowledge; aware or informed of something.
He was *cognizant* of all the facts before he made a decision.

coherent   logically connected; consistent; clearly articulated.
They were too distraught to give a *coherent* account of the crash.

cohesion   sticking together.
The *cohesion* of molecules creates surface tension.

coincide   to be identical; correspond exactly.
This year Thanksgiving *coincides* with her birthday.

collaborate   to work together on a project.
The friends decided to *collaborate* on a novel.

collate   to gather together in proper order for binding.
The photocopies have been *collated* and are ready to be stapled.

Group 2

collateral   side by side; parallel; securities for a debt.

> He cited *collateral* court decisions.
> He offered bonds as *collateral* for his loan.

colloquial   having to do with or like conversation; conversational.

> Having only studied formal French, she was unable to understand many of her host's *colloquial* expressions.

colloquy   a conversation, esp. a formal discussion; conference.

> The faculty held a *colloquy* on grading methods.

collusion   a secret agreement for fraudulent or illegal purposes; conspiracy.

> Higher prices were set by *collusion* among all the manufacturers.

commensurate   equal in measure or size.

> He asked for compensation *commensurate* with his work.

commission   to authorize, especially to have someone perform a task or to act in one's place.

> I have *commissioned* a neighbor to collect the mail while I'm away.

commutation   an exchange, substitution; regular travel between home and work.

> His prison sentence was *commuted* to hard labor.
> *Commutation* is a daily routine for most working people.

compel   to force or constrain, as to do something.

> He was *compelled* by law to make restitution.

compensate   to make up for, be a counterbalance to in weight, force.

> Money could not *compensate* for his sufferings.

complement   that which completes or brings to perfection.

> An expensive wardrobe is the *complement* to his impeccable grooming.
> A *complement* of twelve citizens made up the jury.

compliant   complying or tending to comply; yielding.

> A *compliant* person may gain popularity at the cost of character.

complicity   the fact or state of being an accomplice; partnership in wrongdoing.

> By withholding evidence she became guilty of *complicity* in the crime.

comprehensible   able to be understood or comprehended; intelligible.

The episode was only *comprehensible* to those who knew the story thus far.

comprise   to include; be made up of; consist of; contain.

The test will be *comprised* of the subject matter of the previous lessons.

compulsory   compelling; coercive; required; forced.

Attendance is *compulsory* unless one has a medical excuse.

compunction   a sharp feeling of uneasiness brought on by a sense of guilt; a twinge of conscience; remorse.

He showed no *compunction* over his carelessness.

concede   to admit as true or valid; acknowledge.

When the candidate realized she could not win, she *conceded* gracefully.

concentric   with the same center.

The orbits of the planets are *concentric*..

concept   an idea or thought, esp. a generalized idea of a class of objects; abstract notion.

The *concept* that all individuals have inherent and inalienable rights is basic to our political philosophy.

conception   the beginning of some process or chain of events; mental image.

The *conception* of the plan was originally his.

concerted   mutually agreed upon; made or done together; combined.

The *concerted* plan of action was carried out by all the parties involved.

conciliate   to gain by friendly acts.

The adjustor's task is to *conciliate* the client with a legitimate complaint.

concise   brief and to the point; short and clear.

A précis must be *concise* yet cover the topic.

concomitant   accompanying; attendant.

Due consideration must be given to *concomitant* conditions.

concurrent   occuring or happening at the same time; existing together.

Concurrent action by the police and welfare authorities reduced juvenile crime.

Group 3

condole   to express sympathy; mourn in sympathy; commiserate.

His friends gather to *condole* his loss.

condone   to forgive; pardon; overlook.

The law will not *condone* an act on the plea that the culprit was intoxicated.

conducive   that which conduces or contributes; leading to; helping.

The waterbed was *conducive* to a restful sleep.

conduit   a pipe or channel.

The cables were inserted into a *conduit*.

confiscate   to seize; appropriate for the public treasury, usually as a penalty.

The government has no right to *confiscate* private property without just compensation.

conflagration   a large destructive fire.

New York City was almost destroyed in the 1835 *conflagration*.

conformity   the condition or fact of being in harmony; agreement; correspondence; congruity; similarity.

In *conformity* with the rule, the meeting was adjourned.

confute   to prove to be in error or false; to overwhelm by argument or proof.

His logical rebuttal *confuted* the reasoning of the opposition.

congeal   to solidify or thicken by cooling or freezing; to curdle.

The horrible scene *congealed* his blood.

congenital   inherent; dating from birth; resulting from or developing in one's prenatal environment.

The patient's tendency to schizophrenia is *congenital*.

congruent   in agreement; in harmony; corresponding.

Congruent figures coincide entirely throughout.

conjecture   an inference, theory, or prediction based on guesswork.

He *conjectured* that vocabulary questions would appear on the test.

conscientious   honest, faithful to duty or to what is right showing care and precision; painstaking.

He is *conscientious* in his work and so has won the trust of his employers.

consonance   harmony or agreement of elements or parts; accord.
>   Their *consonance* of opinion in all matters made for a peaceful household.

constrain   to force; compel; oblige.
>   He felt *constrained* to make a full confession.

construe   to analyze; interpret.
>   His attitude was *construed* as one of opposition to the proposal.

contentious   always ready to argue; quarrelsome.
>   One *contentious* student can ruin a debate.

contiguous   near, adjacent, next to, adjoining.
>   Alaska is not *contiguous* to other states of the United States.

contingent   unpredictable because dependent on chance.
>   His plans were *contingent* upon the check's arriving on time.

contort   to twist or wrench out of shape; to distort violently.
>   Rage *contorted* her features into a frightening mask.

contract   a formal agreement, usually written; a compact, convenant.
>   The company signed a *contract* to operate a bookstore on campus.

contravene   to go against; oppose; conflict with; violate.
>   His actions *contravene* the policy set by the Board.

contrive   to think; scheme; devise; plan.
>   They *contrived* a way to fix the unit using old parts.

controversy   discussion of a question in which opposing opinions clash; debate; disputation.
>   A *controversy* arose over whether to use the funds for highway improvement or for mass transit.

convene   gather together, assemble.
>   The graduates will *convene* on the campus.

Group 4

converge   move nearer together, head for one point, place, purpose, or result.
>   The flock *converged* on the seeded field.

conversant   familiar; acquainted with; versed in; having knowledge of.
>   The accountant is *conversant* with the tax laws.

convivial   gay, festive.

Class reunions are *convivial* affairs.

convoke   summon; call together; convene.

The conference was *convoked* to consider amending the constitution of the organization.

copious   plentiful; abundant.

The table was *copiously* set.

corporal   of the body.

Corporal punishment of children in public schools is bitterly resented by many parents.

corpulent   stout; fleshy; obese.

The *corpulent* individual must choose his clothes with great care.

correlation   mutual relation, connectedness.

The doctor explained the *correlation* between smoking and lung disease.

corrigible   capable of being corrected, improved, or reformed.

Corrigible offenders should be separated from hardened criminals.

corroborate   to make the validity of something more certain; confirm; bolster; support.

Laws of evidence require that evidence of a crime must be *corroborated* by other circumstances.

cosmopolitan   belonging to all portions of the world; not national or local.

New York is a *cosmopolitan* city, but many midwest cities are not.

countermand   to cancel or revoke an order or command.

The wise executive will not hesitate to *countermand* an unwise order.

covert   hidden; secret, concealed; disguised; or surreptitious.

To avoid a public outcry, the president ordered a *covert* military action and publicly denied that he was sending combat troops.

credence   faith, belief, esp. in the reports or testimony of another.

One could have little *credence* in the word of a known swindler.

credible   worthy or able to be believed; reliable.

The tale, though unusual, was entirely *credible,* considering the physical evidence.

credulous   inclined to believe on slight evidence; easily convinced.

The *credulous* woman followed every instruction of the fortuneteller.

culpable   faulty, deserving of blame.

The *culpable* parties should not escape punishment.

cursory   superficial; hurried; hasty.

Cursory examination of the scene revealed little information.

curtail   to cut short; abridge, reduce.

Classes were reduced to *curtail* teaching costs.

dearth   scarcity; famine.

A *dearth* of water can create a desert in a few years.

debase   to make lower in value, quality, character, dignity; cheapen.

Do not *debase* yourself by answering him.

debate   to argue formally for and against.

The candidate challenged the incumbent to *debate* the issues on television.

debauch   to lead astray morally; deprave; corrupt.

The temptations they offered could not *debauch* her.

debilitate   enfeeble; weaken; enervate.

Constant excesses will *debilitate* even the strongest constitution.

deceive   to trick; be false to; to betray.

They *deceived* us by telling us that our donations would be used to provide food to the needy; in reality, the money was used to supply guns to the rebels.

Group 5

decimate   to destroy or kill a large part of.

The Black Death had *decimated* the town.

decry   to depreciate officially.

Critics *decry* the lack of emotion on the stage.

deduce   to infer by logical reasoning; reason out or conclude from known facts or general principles.

From the facts presented, we *deduce* this conclusion.

deduct   to take away; subtract.

Because the package was damaged, the seller *deducted* two dollars from the price.

deference   courteous regard or respect.

Out of *deference* to her age, we rose when she entered.

defile   to profane or sully, as a person's name.

A man is not allowed to wear shoes in a mosque, lest he *defile* it.

defunct   no longer living or existing; dead or extinct.

The business has been *defunct* since the big fire.

degenerate   having sunk below a former or normal condition, character; deteriorated.

The discussion eventually *degenerated* into a shouting match.

degrade   to lower in rank or status, as in punishing; demote.

The celebrity refused interviews, feeling that it was *degrading* to have her personal life publicly discussed.

deify   to make a god of; rank among the gods.

They would *deify* Caesar.

delegate   a person authorized or sent to speak and act for others; representative, as at a convention.

Since I will be unable to attend the conference, I have *delegated* my assistant to represent me.

delete   to blot out; destroy.

The proofreader *deleted* the superfluous word.

deleterious   harmful to health or well-being; injurious.

DDT, when taken internally, has a *deleterious* effect on the body.

delineate   to trace the outline of; sketch out.

They asked him to *delineate* the areas where play was permitted.

demagogue   a person who tries to stir up the people by appeals to emotion and prejudice in order to win them over quickly and so gain power.

Hitler was a *demagogue*.

demean   degrade, debase.

Could you *demean* yourself by joining in their crude pastimes?

demote   to lower in status or character.

He was stripped of his rank and *demoted* to private.

demur to hesitate because of one's doubts or objections, have scruples; object.

Once he *demurred*, we knew we had the advantage of additional time to prepare.

demure affectedly modest or shy; coy.

The *demure* maiden was an object of their admiration, but not their affection.

denigrate to disparage the character of; defame.

The lawyer tried to *denigrate* the character of the witness by implying that he was a liar.

deplete to empty wholly or partly.

At the present rates of consumption, the known reserves will be *depleted* before the end of the century.

deplore to be regretful or sorry about; lament.

Pacifists *deplore* violence even on behalf of a just cause.

deprecate to depreciate; belittle.

Do not *deprecate* what you cannot understand.

depreciate to reduce in value or price.

Property will *depreciate* rapidly unless kept in good repair.

depredation the act or an instance of robbing, plundering, or laying waste.

The *depredations* of the Huns left a bloody path across the continent.

Group 6

deride to laugh at in contempt or scorn; make fun of; ridicule.

Many would *deride* the street-corner preacher.

derogatory disparaging.

His *derogatory* remarks hid feelings of envy.

descry to look for and discover; detect.

In the distance we could *descry* a small cabin.

desecrate to take away the sacredness of; treat as not sacred; profane.

Hoodlums attempted to *desecrate* the cemetery.

designate to name for an office or duty, appoint.

We will rendezvous at the time and place *designated* on the sheet.

destitute   lacking the necessities of life; living in complete poverty.
   Even the most *destitute* person has hope for the future.

desultory   lacking direct relevancy; random; incidental.
   Desultory reading will seldom create a well-read individual; reading must
   be planned.

deterrent   a thing or factor that deters.
   The absolute certainty of apprehension is a powerful *deterrent* to crime.

detract   take or draw away.
   The old-fashioned engraving *detracted* from the value of the piece of jewelry.

deviate   to turn aside.
   The honest man will never *deviate* from the path of rectitude.

devious   not in a straight path; roundabout; winding.
   When no one would tell her anything, she resorted to *devious* means to
   uncover the truth.

devise   to work out or create by thinking; contrive; plan; invent.
   I will *devise* a plan of escape.

devolve   to pass to another or others; said of duties, responsibilities.
   The duties of the position *devolved* upon the new sales manager.

dictum   a statement or saying; specif. a formal statement of fact, opinion, principle
   or of one's will or judgment; pronouncement.
   The professor's *dictum* ended the debate.

didactic   used or intended for teaching or instruction.
   The *didactic* approach may be well suited for a text book but should be
   avoided in books aimed at the general public.

diffidence   lack of confidence in oneself, marked by a hesitancy to assert oneself;
   shyness.
   His *diffidence* caused him to miss many opportunities.

diffuse   to spread out or disperse; not concentrated.
   When the bottle broke, the fragrance *diffused* throughout the room.

digress   to depart temporarily from the main subject in talking or writing; ramble.
   To *digress* from the main topic may lend interest to a theme, but at the
   cost of its unity.

dilate   to become wider or larger; swell.
   Some drugs will cause the pupil of the eye to *dilate*.

dilatory   inclined to delay; slow or late in doing things.

>   The filibuster is an effective legislative tool in *dilatory* campaigns.

dilemma   any situation in which one must choose between unpleasant alternatives.

>   Even a wrong decision may be preferable to remaining in a *dilemma*.

discernible   to perceive or recognize the difference.

>   The other cars were barely *discernible* in the fog.

disclaim   to give up or renounce any claim to or connection with.

>   In order to obtain United States citizenship, one must *disclaim* any title or rank of nobility from another nation.

disconcert   to upset the composure of; embarrass, confuse.

>   An apathetic audience may *disconcert* even the most experienced performer.

discordant   not in harmony; dissonant; clashing.

>   The *discordant* cries of wild birds may make summer vacationers long for the familiar sounds of the city.

Group 7

discreet   careful about what one says or does; prudent, esp., keeping silent or preserving confidences when necessary.

>   She countered the rude question with a soft-spoken and *discreet* denial.

discrete   separate and distinct; not attached to others; unrelated.

>   The process is divided into six *discrete* steps.

discursive   wandering from one topic to another; skimming over many apparently unconnected subjects; rambling; desultory; digressive.

>   A debater must check the tendency to *discursive* remarks.

disdain   to regard or treat as unworthy or beneath one's dignity; specif. to refuse or reject with aloof contempt or scorn.

>   Many beginners *disdain* a lowly job that might in time lead to the position they desire.

disinterested   not influenced by personal interest or selfish motives; impartial; unbiased.

>   A *disinterested* witness is one who has no personal involvement in the outcome of the matter under dispute.

disjoin   to undo the joining of; separate; detach.

>   The links of the chain were *disjoined*.

disparage   to speak slightingly of; show disrespect for; belittle.

>   A teacher who *disparages* the efforts of beginners in her subject is not helping them.

disparity   inequality or difference as in rank, amount or quality.

   A *disparity* in age need not mean an incompatible marriage.

dispel   to scatter and drive away; cause to banish; disperse.

   The good-humored joke *dispelled* the tension in the room.

disputation   discussion marked by formal debate, often as an exercise.

   In his *disputation*, he defended the theories expressed in his paper.

disquieting   restless; uneasy.

   There have been *disquieting* reports of a buildup of forces along the border.

dissemble   to pretend to be in a state of; simulate; feign.

   A skillful publicity man will *dissemble* his propaganda to appear as impartial information.

disseminate   to scatter far and wide; spread abroad, as if sowing; promulgate widely.

   With missionary zeal, they *disseminated* the literature about the new religion.

dissension   a difference of opinion; disagreement or esp., violent quarreling or wrangling.

   There was *dissension* among the delegates about which candidate to support.

dissolute   dissipated and immoral; profligate; debauched.

   The *dissolute* young man was soon without friends or reputation.

dissonant   opposing in opinion, temperment; incompatible; incongruous.

   Much contemporary music seems *dissonant* to unaccustomed ears.

dissuade   to advise against.

   His friends *dissuaded* him from that unwise plan of action.

distend   to stretch.

   If you *distend* a balloon beyond a certain point, it will break.

distortion   a distorting or being distorted.

   The *distortions* of the historians left little of the man's true character for posterity.

distract   to draw away in another direction; divert.

   The loud crash *distracted* the attention of the students.

distraught   driven mad; crazed.

   The young woman, *distraught* at the tragedy of her husband's death, threatened suicide.

diverge to go or move in different directions from a common point; branch off.
> The map showed a main lode with thin veins *diverging* in all directions.

diversity variety.
> A university should encourage a *diversity* of opinion among the faculty.

divest to strip.
> After the court martial, he was *divested* of his rank and decorations.

divisive causing division, esp. causing disagreement or dissension.
> The issue of abortion, on which people hold deep and morally-based convictions, was *divisive* to the movement.

Group 8

divulge to make public.
> Newspapermen have long fought the courts for the right not to *divulge* their sources of information.

docile easily taught.
> The child was *docile* until he discovered his mother was gone.

dogmatic stating opinion in a positive or arrogant manner.
> His *dogmatic* statements were not supported by evidence.

dormant sleeping.
> Perennial flowers such as irises remain *dormant* every winter and burgeon in the spring.

dubious causing doubt; ambiguous; vague.
> He had the *dubious* distinction of being the best liar at the school.

ductile able to be stretched, drawn out or hammered thin without breaking.
> The *ductile* quality of gold makes it possible to manufacture fine gold leaf for artists' frames.

duplicity hypocritical cunning or deception; double-dealing.
> The *duplicity* of the marketplace may shock the naive.

dynamic energetic, forceful; vigorous.
> A *dynamic* leader can inspire followers with enthusiasm and confidence.

eclectic selecting from various systems, doctrines, or sources.
> His *eclectic* record collection included everything from Bach to rock.

ecology the branch of biology that deals with the relations between living organisms and their environment.
> Persons concerned about *ecology* are worried about the pollution of the earth's environment and the effect this will have on life.

ecstasy   a state of being overpowered by emotion, as by joy, grief, or passion.
The lovers were in *ecstasy* just in touching each other's hands.

edict   an official public proclamation or order issued by authority; decree.
The *edict* issued by the junta dissolved the government.

edify   to instruct, esp. to instruct or improve morally or spiritually; enlighten.
Some teachers *edify*; others merely try.

educe   draw out, elicit.
Can you *educe* any information from her notes?

effect   (v.) to bring about. (n.) a result.
New regulations have *effected* a shift in policy on applications.
The headache was an *effect* of sinus congestion.

efficacious   producing or capable of producing the desired effect; having the intended result; effective.
The drug is *efficacious* in the treatment of malaria.

effusive   pouring out or forth; overflowing.
Her *effusive* greeting seemed overdone.

egocentric   viewing everything in relation to oneself; self-centered.
The *egocentric* individual has little regard for the feelings of others.

egotism   constant, excessive reference to oneself in speaking or writing.
His *egotism* demanded that he always be the center of attention.

egress   a way out; exit.
Barnum put the sign *"egress"* on the door so that the crowd would move on, expecting to see another exhibit.

elate   to raise the spirits of; make very proud, happy, or joyful.
A grade of 100% will *elate* any student.

elicit   to draw forth; evoke.
Her direct question only *elicited* further evasions.

elucidate   to make clear; explain.
The explanation served to confuse rather than to *elucidate.*

elude   to avoid or escape from by quickness and cunning; evade.
The thief *eluded* the police by darting into a crowded theater.

elusive   hard to grasp or retain mentally; baffling.
Because the problem is so complex, a definitive solution seems *elusive.*

Module 2: *Chastisement–Elusive*

Challenge 61

Choose the word or phrase that means most nearly the same as the key word or the italicized word.

1. The word *diversity* means most nearly
   a. similarity
   b. value
   c. triviality
   d. variety

2. The word *divergent* means most nearly
   a. simultaneous
   b. differing
   c. approaching
   d. parallel

3. The driver *conceded* that he was at fault. The word *conceded* means most nearly
   a. denied
   b. explained
   c. implied
   d. admitted

4. The word *cognizant* means most nearly
   a. rare
   b. reluctant
   c. aware
   d. haphazard

5. corroboration
   a. expenditure
   b. compilation
   c. confirmation
   d. reduction

6. dogmatic
   a. manual
   b. doctrinaire
   c. canine
   d. unprincipled

7. desultory
   a. errant
   b. dejected
   c. aimless
   d. destitute

8. dilatory
   a. slow
   b. enlarged
   c. aimless
   d. expansive

9. congruent
   a. noisy
   b. agreeing
   c. quarrelsome
   d. sticky

10. degraded
    a. unassorted
    b. declassified
    c. receded
    d. debased

11. congenital
    a. harmonious
    b. sympathetic
    c. inherent
    d. fringed

12. deprecate
    a. lower the worth
    b. express disapproval
    c. apologize for
    d. applaud

13. culpable
    a. dangerous
    b. soft
    c. blameworthy
    d. easily perceived

14. coherent
    a. not clear
    b. courteous
    c. specific
    d. logically related

15. edify
    a. proclaim
    b. revise
    c. whirl
    d. enlighten

Challenge 62

Choose the word or phrase that is most opposite in meaning to the given word.

1. condone
   a. condemn
   b. disregard
   c. punish
   d. mistake

2. dilatory
   a. hairy
   b. happy-go-lucky
   c. ruined
   d. punctual

3. cursory
   a. thorough
   b. impolite
   c. honest
   d. quickly

4. derisive
   a. dividing
   b. furnishing
   c. reflecting
   d. laudatory

5. debilitate
   a. encourage
   b. insinuate
   c. prepare
   d. strengthen

6. eclectic
   a. brilliant
   b. exclusive
   c. pastoral poem
   d. conclusive

7. deride
   a. fly
   b. praise
   c. amend
   d. admit

8. discern
   a. misperceive
   b. emit
   c. expand
   d. deploy

9. discrete
   a. prudent
   b. joined
   c. crooked
   d. stunted

10. dissonance
    a. disapproval
    b. disaster
    c. harmony
    d. disparity

11. disparage
    a. applaud
    b. degrade
    c. erase
    d. reform

12. conversant
    a. terse
    b. pushy
    c. convinced
    d. unfamiliar

13. corroborate
    a. correct
    b. strengthen
    c. broaden
    d. undermine

14. derogatory
    a. uneven
    b. equal
    c. opposite
    d. flattering

15. depredation
    a. plethora
    b. gross
    c. restoration
    d. glamour

Module 3: *Embody–Juxtaposition*

Group 1

embody   to make part of an organized whole; incorporate.
> He tried to *embody* his ideas in the theme.

emissary   person or agent, esp. a secret agent, sent on a specific mission.
> The rebels sent an *emissary* to negotiate a truce.

empathy   the projection of one's own personality onto an object, with the attribution to the object of one's own emotions or responses, etc.
> Her *empathy* with her brother was very strong; she generally knew what her sibling was feeling without his having to explain.

employ   to make use of; use.
> The artist *employed* charcoal in many of her sketches.

enact   to make into law, pass; decree; ordain.
> A bill was *enacted* lowering the voting age to eighteen.

endogenous   developing from within; originating internally.
> An ulcer is usually *endogenous*.

enervate   weaken physically, mentally, or morally; devitalize; debilitate.
> A poor diet will *enervate* a person.

enforce   to give force to; urge.
> Because of the holiday, parking restrictions are not being *enforced* today.

engender   to beget.
> Angry words may *engender* strife.

engross   to take the entire attention of; occupy wholly; absorb.
> He was so *engrossed* in his hobbies that he neglected his studies.

engulf   to swallow up; overwhelm.
> The rising waters *engulfed* the village.

enlighten   reveal truths to; free from ignorance, prejudice, or superstition.
> No *enlightened* society could condone the exploitation of children as it was once practiced in American industry.

enmity   the bitter attitude or feelings of an enemy as of mutual enemies; hostility; antagonism.
> The *enmity* between China and Vietnam is traditional and unabated.

ensnare   to catch, as in a snare; trap.

He was *ensnared* in the fabric of his lies.

ensue   come afterward; follow immediately.

One person raised an objection and a long argument *ensued*.

ephemeral   short-lived; transitory.

Ephemeral pleasures may leave lasting memories.

epilogue   a closing section added to a novel or play; providing further comment, interpretation, or information.

The *epilogue* is delivered at the conclusion of the drama.

equanimity   the quality of remaining calm and undisturbed; evenness of mind or temper; composure.

Adversity could not disturb his *equanimity*.

equivocal   that can have more than one interpretation; having two or more meanings; purposely vague, misleading, or ambiguous.

His *equivocal* statements left us in doubt as to his real intentions.

erode   to eat into; wear away; disintegrate.

The glaciers *eroded* the land, leaving deep valleys.

erudite   having or showing a wide knowledge gained from reading.

The *erudite* person may find it difficult to communicate his thoughts to those less educated.

erupt   to burst forth or out, as from some restraint.

The volcano *erupted* streams of lava.

eschew   to keep away from; shun; avoid.

She *eschewed* any social activities and lived in total seclusion.

esoteric   intended for or understood by only a chosen few, as an inner group of disciples or initiates; said of ideas, doctrines, literatures.

The *esoteric* rites of the fraternity were held sacred by the members.

ethereal   not earthly; heavenly; celestial.

The heroine of his book was endowed with *ethereal* beauty.

Group 2

ethical   conforming to the standards of conduct of a given profession or group.

Although many members of his administration were corrupt, he adhered to strong *ethical* principles.

ethnic   designating or belonging to any of the basic groups or divisions of mankind or of a heterogeneous population, as distinguished by customs, characteristics, or common history.

> Of all the *ethnic* foods available in this city, Italian pizza and Middle Eastern falafel are the most popular.

eugenic   relating to the bearing of sound offspring.

> *Eugenics* has provided us with improved animals in every class except the human race.

eulogy   speech or writing in praise of a person who has recently died.

> He asked that no *eulogy* be delivered at his funeral.

euphemism   an inoffensive word or phrase substituted for a more straightforward one.

> Like many other people he used "gone" and "passed away" as *euphemisms* for "dead."

euphonic   of or having to do with euphony; pleasant sounding.

> Her *euphonic* singing had a soothing effect on the guests.

euphoria   a feeling of vigor, well-being, or high spirits.

> Their *euphoria* at being the first to ever climb the mountain was heightened by their narrow escape from death.

euthanasia   any easy and painless death.

> *Euthanasia* is not legal.

evasion   a subterfuge; an avoiding; any way of doing this.

> His indirect answers were an attempt at *evasion*.

evince   to show plainly; indicate; make manifest.

> His curt reply *evinced* his short temper.

evolution   a gradual change; a result or product of this.

> Through the discovery of ancient bones and artifacts, anthropologists hope to chart the *evolution* of the human species.

exacerbate   to exasperate; annoy; irritate; embitter.

> A generous portion of french fries is sure to *exacerbate* an upset stomach.

exceed   to go or be beyond.

> The business's profits for this year *exceeded* last year's profits by $16,000.

except   make an exception of; exclude; omit.

> He *excepted* the damaging remarks from his speech.

exclude   to refuse to admit, consider, or include; shut out; keep from entering, happening or being; reject; bar.
> The children made a pact that all adults were to be *excluded* from the clubhouse.

excoriate   to strip, scratch or rub off the skin of; flay, abrade, chafe, etc.; denounce harshly.
> The principal *excoriated* the student as a juvenile delinquent.

execrable   very inferior; of poorest quality.
> Although her acting was *execrable,* she looked so good on stage that the audience applauded.

execrate   to loathe; detest; abhor.
> The captors who had lost all sense of humanity deserved to be *execrated.*

exempt   to free from a rule of obligation which applies to others; excuse; release.
> Having broken his leg, the child was *exempt* from gym for the rest of the term.

exhibit   to present or expose to view; show; display.
> The paintings were *exhibited* in the municipal museum.

exhort   to urge by advice or warning.
> He *exhorted* the mob to attack the station.

exogenous   developing from without; originating externally.
> His delusions seemed to have no internal cause and were thus termed *exogenous.*

exonerate   to free from a charge or imputation of guilt; declare or prove blameless; exculpate.
> The confession of one prisoner *exonerated* the other suspects.

exorbitant   excessive, going beyond what is reasonable, just, proper, usual.
> The *exorbitant* rates of the moneylenders kept the peasants in a state of poverty.

expansible   that which can be expanded.
> Bodies are not *expansible* in proportion to their weight.

Group 3

expedient   useful for effecting a desired result; suited to the circumstances or the occasion; advantageous; convenient.
> Under pressure to reduce the deficit, the mayor found it *expedient* to cut funds for social services.

expel   to drive out by force; force out; eject.

When a balloon bursts, the air is *expelled* in a rush.

expertise   the skill, knowledge, or judgment of an expert.

The *expertise* with which he handled the animal delighted the spectators.

explicate   to make clear; explain fully.

He could not *explicate* a philosophy that depended on doing evil.

exploit   to make use of; turn to account; utilize productively.

Some employers *exploit* the labor of illegal immigrants, who are afraid to complain about long hours and substandard wages.

expostulate   to reason with a person earnestly, objecting to his actions or intentions; remonstrate.

He *expostulated* loudly and clearly with his students about their poor working habits.

expulsion   an expelling or forcing out, or the condition of being expelled.

The *expulsion* of the students from the university was unfair.

expurgate   to remove passages considered obscene or otherwise objectionable (from a book, etc.).

The censors *expurgated* the portions of the book they considered obscene.

extemporaneous   made, done, or spoken without any preparation; unpremeditated; offhand.

The speaker who was expected to make the presentation didn't show up, so he gave an *extemporaneous* speech.

extenuate   to lessen or seem to lessen the seriousness of by giving excuses or serving as an excuse.

His abrupt rudeness was *extenuated* by his distraught state of mind; no one could blame him for it.

extirpate   to destroy or remove completely; exterminate; abolish.

The soldier threatened to *extirpate* the entire village if they refused to surrender.

extricate   to set free; release from an entanglement.

Carefully removing each prickly branch, she *extricated* herself from the briars.

extrinsic   being, coming, or acting from the outside; extraneous.

Her complaints about one particular teacher are *extrinsic* to an evaluation of the program as a whole.

extrude   to push or force out, expel.

   The volcanic upheaval *extruded* molten lava over a vast area.

facile   acting; working or done easily, or in a quick smooth way; fluent; ready.

   He never turned down an opportunity to make a speech because he was such a *facile* orator.

facilitate   to make easy or easier.

   This piece of machinery will *facilitate* production.

facility   ease of doing or making; absence of difficulty.

   Her *facility* in reading several languages made her ideal for the cataloguing job.

fallacious   misleading or deceptive; causing disappointment; delusive.

   His arguments were transparently *fallacious*.

fallible   liable to be mistaken or deceived in judgment.

   All men are *fallible*.

fatuous   complacently stupid or inane; silly; foolish.

   Insisting on a Cadillac you can't afford is *fatuous*.

feasible   capable of being done or carried out; practicable; possible.

   It is *feasible* to complete the project by July.

feckless   weak, ineffective.

   A *feckless* soldier is a liability to his outfit.

finite   having measurable or definable limits; not infinite.

   There were only a *finite* number of men to be considered.

flammable   easily set on fire; that will burn readily or quickly.

   They were careful to keep the material away from the sparks because it was *flammable*.

flaunt   to make gaudy; ostentatious; a conspicuous, impudent, or defiant display.

   Flaunting expensive jewelry in public may be an invitation to robbery.

Group 4

flout   to be scornful; show contempt; jeer; scoff.

   He *flouted* public opinion by appearing with his lover in public.

fluctuate   to be continually changing or varying in an irregular way.

> *Fluctuations* in stock market prices create many paper losses and profits.

foreclose   to deprive of the right to redeem a mortgage when payments have not been kept up.

> The bank *foreclosed* the mortgage and repossessed the house, putting it up for sale.

foresight   a looking forward.

> She had the *foresight* to realize that the restaurant would be busy, so she called ahead for reservations.

garrulous   talking much or too much about unimportant things; loquacious.

> She was so *garrulous* that she said everything at least three times.

gauche   lacking grace, esp. social grace; awkward; tactless.

> It is considered *gauche* to ask acquaintances how much they earn or how much they paid for something.

genealogy   the science or study of family descent.

> They were able to trace their *genealogy* back four generations to a small village in Sicily.

generalization   a general idea or statement, resulting from this; inference; applied generally.

> *Generalizations* are apt to be as dangerous as they are tempting.

generate   to procreate, beget, produce.

> Every animal *generates* its own species.

generic   of or characteristic of a genus.

> The *generic* characteristics of each animal enable us to distinguish them.

genial   cheerful; friendly; sympathetic; amiable.

> The president's rotund and *genial* face made him the perfect Santa Claus.

geriatrics   branch of medicine that deals with the diseases and hygiene of old age.

> Our longer life span in modern times makes the study of *geriatrics* a necessity.

germane   pertinent; truly relevant; to the point.

> The facts were not *germane* to the argument.

gratuitous   given or received without charge or payment; free.

> His *gratuitous* insults were resented very highly.

gratuity   a gift of money, esp. that given over payment due for a service rendered; tip.

He left a *gratuity* for the chambermaid.

gregarious   fond of the company of others; sociable.

They are a *gregarious* couple who cultivate many friendships among diverse people.

gyrate   to turn, whirl.

The tornado *gyrates* about a central point.

habitable   fit to be lived in.

The climate of the North Pole makes it scarcely *habitable*.

heinous   outrageously evil or wicked; abominable.

The deed was so *heinous* that everyone despised him for it.

helix   a spiral; to turn round.

The wire was wound into a *helix*.

herald   a person who proclaims or announces significant news; often used as the name of a newspaper.

Crocuses *herald* the advent of spring.

herbivorous   feeding on plants.

A vegetarian is *herbivorous*.

heterodox   departing from or opposed to the usual beliefs or established doctrines; esp. in religion; inclining toward heresy; unorthodox.

Her *heterodox* opinions and outlandish behavior earned her a reputation as an eccentric.

heterogeneous   of different origin; not from the same source, individual, or species.

The school favored *heterogeneous* groupings, so there was a very wide range of ability and achievement in every class.

hindsight   ability to see after the event what should have been done.

With *hindsight* I realize that everything she said to me was true, though I could not accept it at the time.

Group 5

holocaust   great or total destruction of life, esp. by fire.

As the fire raged out of control, thousands of lives were lost in the *holocaust*.

holograph   written entirely in the handwriting of the person under whose name it appears.

A *holograph* attached to a will needs no witnesses.

homicide   any killing of one person by another.

Killing in self-defense is considered justifiable *homicide*.

homogeneous   the same in structure and quality; similar or identical.

The entering class was fairly *homogeneous*; nearly all the students were the same age and from similar middle-class homes.

hortatory   serving to encourage or urge to good deeds.

With his *hortatory* speech, the orator incited his listeners to riot.

humanities   languages and literature, esp. the classical Greek and Latin.

The essence of the *humanities* is a concern with human nature, experience, and relationships.

hydrous   containing water, esp. water of crystallization or hydration, as in certain mineral and chemical compounds.

Watermelon is a *hydrous* gourd.

hyperbole   exaggeration for effect, not meant to be taken literally.

"He was as big as a house" is an example of *hyperbole*.

hypertension   abnormally high blood pressure or a disease of which it is the chief sign.

Hypertension is often a cause of serious disease.

hypothesis   an unproved theory, proposition or supposition.

She started with the *hypothesis* that the earth was spheroid and concluded it would be possible to go east by sailing west.

ideologue   a student of or expert in the study of ideas; exponent of a specific ideology.

The communist *ideologue* argued that the state was more important than any individual.

ideology   the doctrines, opinions, or way of thinking of an individual or class.

The communist *ideology* holds the State important and the individual inconsequential.

igneous   produced by the action of fire; specif. formed by volcanic action or intense heat, as rocks solidified from molten magma at or below the surface of the earth.

The Palisades of the Hudson Valley are of *igneous* origin.

ignoble   not noble in character or quality; dishonorable; mean.

The *ignoble* purpose of his slander multiplied the crime.

ignominious   discrediting, disgraceful.

His *ignominious* activities could lead only to his removal from office.

illegible   very difficult or impossible to read because badly written, printed, or faded.

The letter was so water stained that the handwriting was *illegible*.

illicit   not allowed by law, custom, or rule.

Illicit love is the root of many divorce actions.

illuminate   to give light to; light up.

The editor's notes *illuminated* the more obscure passages in the text.

impassioned   filled with passion; having or showing strong feeling; passionate; fiery; ardent.

The *impassioned* performance of the actor was thoroughly enjoyable.

impeccable   not liable to sin or wrongdoing.

Successful comedy depends on *impeccable* timing.

impecunious   having no money; poor; penniless.

His *impecunious* aunt was a drain on his purse.

impede   to bar or hinder the progress of; obstruct or delay.

The flying shrapnel *impeded* the progress of the troops.

impediment   an impeding or being impeded; obstruction.

The loss of two front teeth caused a speech *impediment*.

impel   to push into motion, to drive.

Although she was not personally involved, her sense of justice *impelled* her to speak out.

imperative   absolutely necessary; urgent; compelling.

This is an emergency; it is *imperative* that I reach them at once.

Group 6

imperturbable   that cannot be disconcerted, disturbed, or excited; impassive.

His poker face was aided by an *imperturbable* nature.

impervious   incapable of being passed through or penetrated.
> Heavy cardboard is *impervious* to light.

impetuous   acting or done suddenly with little thought; rash; impulsive.
> The *impetuous* action often leads to trouble.

importune   ask for urgently; demand.
> Do not *importune* me for what you can earn so easily.

impotent   lacking physical strength; weak.
> The disease left him *impotent* even to walk across the room.

imprecation   a curse.
> He uttered an *imprecation* that sent shudders through the superstitious mob.

imprecise   not precise, exact, or definite; vague.
> The description was *imprecise* because the witness had had only a fleeting glimpse of the man.

impute   to attribute to another; charge with; ascribe.
> The difficulties were *imputed* to his negligence.

inadvertence   the quality of being inadvertent; an instant of this; oversight; mistake.
> The bookkeeper's *inadvertence* caused several checks to be returned unpaid.

inalienable   that may not be taken away or transferred.
> We are endowed with certain *inalienable* rights.

inception   the act of beginning; start; commencement.
> The scheme was harebrained from its *inception*; it was no surprise when it was abandoned.

incessant   never ceasing; continuing or being repeated without stopping or in a way that seems endless; constant.
> The *incessant* rain kept the children indoors all day.

incision   the act or result of incising; cut; gash.
> The surgeon made an *incision* above the navel.

incognito   a disguise assumed.
> The prince traveled *incognito*.

incorrigible   that cannot be corrected, improved, or reformed, esp. because firmly established as a habit.

Some delinquents are *incorrigible.*

inculcate   to impress upon the mind by frequent repetition or persistent urging.

From earliest childhood they had been *inculcated* with the tenets of the community's belief.

inculpate   to blame.

To *inculpate* others in your troubles may bring some ego satisfaction, but it never brings a solution.

incur   to come into or acquire.

The debts *incurred* in the legal proceedings were to be paid off in monthly installments.

indict   to charge with the commission of a crime.

The Grand Jury issues an *indictment.*

indigenous   existing, growing, or produced naturally in a region or country; belonging as a native.

The *indigenous* trees of the Rockies are largely evergreens.

indoctrinate   to instruct in or imbue with doctrines, theories, beliefs, as of a sect.

Children are sent to Sunday School to be *indoctrinated* in the basic tenets of a particular religion.

indolent   disliking or avoiding work; idle; lazy.

An *indolent* lad never learns much.

indubitable   that cannot be doubted; unquestionable.

That $2 \times 2 = 4$ is *indubitable.*

induct   formally to lead or bring in.

The Army *inducts* 100 men a week in New York.

indurate   hardened; callous or unfeeling.

He was an *indurate* criminal.

Group 7

inept   clumsy; bungling; inefficient.

The basketball team's center is tall and powerful but so physically *inept* that he frequently loses the ball.

inexorable   that cannot be moved or influenced by persuasion or entreaty; unrelenting.

> The *inexorable* logic of history points to a period of decadence for every satisfied nation.

infiltrate   to pass, or cause to pass, through weak places in the enemy lines in order to attack the enemy's flank or rear.

> The radical organization had been *infiltrated* by federal agents who monitored its membership and activities.

infraction   a breaking of a law or pact.

> The building inspector noted several *infractions* of the health and safety codes.

ingenuous   frank; open; candid.

> An *ingenuous* approach is often better than guile.

ingratiate   to bring into another's favor or good graces by conscious effort.

> He tried to *ingratiate* himself with his teacher by bringing her apples.

inherent   existing in someone or something as a natural and inseparable quality, characteristic, or right; innate.

> A love of hunting is *inherent* in cats.

inhibition   a mental or psychological process that restrains or suppresses an action, emotion, or thought.

> *Inhibition* is particularly important for emotional people.

initiation   the ceremony by which a person is initiated into a fraternity or organization.

> The *initiation* of new members into the fraternity will be held soon and the old members can hardly wait.

innocuous   that does not injure or harm; harmless.

> His words were *innocuous*, but his temper vile.

innovation   something newly introduced; new method, custom, or device causing a change in the way of doing things.

> The celebration of the Mass in languages other than Latin is a major 20th-century *innovation* in the Roman Catholic Church.

inquest   a judicial inquiry, as a coroner's investigation of a death.

> The state held an *inquest* to examine the cause of the disaster and determine whether charges should be brought against any parties.

inquisitive   inclined to ask many questions or seek information; eager to learn.

> Private eyes in detective fiction often get into trouble by being too *inquisitive.*

insatiable   constantly wanting more; that which cannot be satisfied or appeased; very greedy.

> His appetite for wealth was *insatiable;* no matter how rich he became, he always craved more.

inscrutable   that cannot be easily understood; incomplete, obscure, or mysterious; unfathomable; enigmatic.

> His face was *inscrutable* when he doubled his bet.

insensate   without sense or feeling; foolish; stupid.

> In his *insensate* rage he did not yet feel the pain of his injury.

insolvent   not enough to pay all debts; bankrupt.

> The corporation was *insolvent* after the loss of the ship.

insubordinate   not submitting to authority; disobedient.

> Ignoring a direct order is an *insubordinate* act with grave consequences.

insure   to contract to be paid or to pay money in the case of loss of (life, property, etc.); to give or take out insurance.

> Bail is set to *insure* the defendant's appearance in court.

intangible   that which cannot be touched; incorporeal; impalpable.

> The company's goodwill among its customers is a genuine but *intangible* asset.

integral   necessary for completeness; essential.

> Alaska is an *integral* part of the United States.

integration   the putting or bringing of parts together into a whole; unification.

> Vertical *integration* results from the merger of companies that perform different operations in the manufacture of a product.

intensive   extreme degree of anything.

> *Intensive* private tutoring is needed to take care of this student's reading problem.

intercede   to plead or make a request in behalf of another or others.

> He asked his preacher to *intercede* with the judge.

intercept   to stop, hinder, or prevent.

> The missile was *intercepted* and destroyed before it reached its target.

Group 8

interdict to prohibit an action or the use of; forbid with authority.

>He issued an *interdict* on carrying arms.

interpolate to alter, enlarge, or corrupt by putting in new words, subject matter.

>The editor *interpolated* the latest news into the proofs.

interregnum an interval between two successive reigns; a time when the country has no sovereign.

>He asked for a regency in the *interregnum*.

intractable hard to manage; unruly or stubborn.

>An *intractable* person is slow to learn a new way of life.

intransigent refusing to compromise, come to an agreement, or be reconciled; uncompromising.

>The *intransigent* attitude of the abolitionists did much to antagonize the South.

intravenous in, or directly into, a vein or veins.

>The patient was given an *intravenous* feeding of glucose because he could not swallow.

intrepid not afraid; bold; fearless; dauntless, very brave.

>The *intrepid* explorers stepped out onto the lunar surface.

intrinsic belonging to the real nature of a thing; not depending on external circumstances; essential; inherent.

>The *intrinsic* value of diamonds lies in their hardness.

introvert to direct upon oneself; introspect.

>The *introvert* makes friends with difficulty; the extrovert makes friends with ease.

inundate to overflow.

>When the craze was at its height, the police were *inundated* with daily reports of UFO sightings.

inverse inverted; in reverse in order or relation; directly opposite.

>Work gets done in direct ratio with the number working, in *inverse* ratio with the amount of chatter involved.

invidious such as to excite ill will, jealousy, or envy; giving offense.

>His tactlessness was *invidious*.

invocation   the act of calling on God, a god, a saint, the muses for blessing, help, inspiration, support, or the like.
   The minister delivered the *invocation* at the beginning of the ceremony.

irony   a method of humorous or subtly sarcastic expression in which the intended meaning of the words used is the direct opposite of their usual sense.
   He said with *irony* that he didn't like vacations because he liked school so much.

irradiate   to heat with radiant energy.
   The heat from the fireplace *irradiated* the room, warming us all.

irreconcilable   ideas or beliefs that cannot be brought into agreement with each other.
   His statements about liking school were *irreconcilable* with the distaste he expressed for books in general.

irritate   to excite to impatience or anger; provoke; annoy; exasperate.
   The harsh cleansers used in the job can *irritate* the skin.

itinerant   traveling from place to place on a circuit.
   The *itinerant* judge heard cases in Somerville on the first Tuesday of the month.

itinerary   a record of a journey.
   Our *itinerary* includes three days in Florence and a week in Rome.

jettison   a throwing overboard of goods to lighten a ship or airplane, esp. in an emergency.
   They had to *jettison* the cargo to lighten the plane.

jocose   joking, humorous, or playful.
   She had the sense not to take his *jocose* teasing seriously.

jollity   the quality or state of being jolly; fun; gaiety.
   The *jollity* of the occasion will always be remembered.

judicial   of judges, law courts, or their functions.
   Chief Justice of the Supreme Court is the highest *judicial* position in the United States.

judicious   having, applying, or showing sound judgment; wise and careful.
   His policy was *judicious* and the results effective.

juxtaposition   to put side by side or close together.
   The *juxtaposition* of the Capitol and White House was avoided in planning the city of Washington to emphasize the separation of the legislature from the executive branch.

Challenge 63

Select the word or phrase that will best complete the meaning of the sentence as a whole.

1. The tendency to be totally absorbed with one's own mental life is called _____.
   a. introspection
   b. acoustics
   c. stimulation
   d. anthropomorphism
   e. introversion

2. His conclusions were so _____ that they helped no one.
   a. imprecise
   b. incalculable
   c. unknown
   d. impecunious
   e. orthodox

3. She was a woman of _____ integrity; no one questioned her standards.
   a. vague
   b. indubitable
   c. suspected
   d. inchoate
   e. mysterious

4. The _____ mediator in the labor talks was known for his record of fairness in similar cases.
   a. lucrative
   b. judicious
   c. serendipitous
   d. phantasmogoric
   e. ludicrous

5. The Political Action Committee sought to _____ the right-wing demonstrators from the more liberal rally.
   a. detain
   b. exclude
   c. deny
   d. exacerbate
   e. propel

6. Because coal is formed when molten material from beneath the earth's surface dries, it is an _____ rock.
   a. indigenous
   b. indispensible
   c. igneous
   d. ignatius
   e. inscrutable

7. The patient's _____ pain could not be alleviated by medication.
   a. bandaged
   b. untraceable
   c. intractable
   d. imperturbable
   e. mild

8. The young socialite, forever seeking the company of other carefree young women, was extremely _____.
   a. gregarious
   b. visible
   c. ungrateful
   d. flippant
   e. ostensive

9. His comments were unnecessary
   and _____; no one could
   understand why he added them.
   a. gracious
   b. gratuitous
   c. grotesque
   d. gregarious
   e. garbled

10. The plate began to _____
    on top of the juggler's pole when
    he shook it gently.

    a. wobble
    b. hang
    c. gallop
    d. gyrate
    e. flutter

11. The vicious attack on the old cou-
    ple was denounced as _____,
    horrible, and unforgivable.
    a. haphazard
    b. holistic
    c. hesitant
    d. happenstance
    e. heinous

12. The old man had the _____
    to save money during his teaching
    career so as not to be dependent
    on irregular Social Security checks
    after his retirement.
    a. thrift
    b. stinginess
    c. foresight
    d. foretelling ability
    e. gumption

13. Because everyone knew she tended
    to exaggerate when she got ex-
    cited, no one took her _____
    seriously.
    a. hyperboles
    b. hypertension
    c. hypotension
    d. hysteria
    e. hilarity

14. A parent tries to _____
    children with sound morals and
    respect for others.
    a. inculcate
    b. calculate
    c. incubate
    d. incarcerate
    e. inoculate

15. According to one school of sci-
    entific thought, man, slowly
    adapting to his changing environ-
    ment, _____ from the
    same species as the ape.
    a. evolved
    b. evoked
    c. everted
    d. reverted
    e. devolved

Module 4: *Kindred–Provocation*

Group 1

kindred   relatives or family; kin; kinfolk.

> Though from diverse backgrounds, they were *kindred* spirits, alike in intellect and ambition.

kinetic   of or resulting from motion.

> *Kinetic* energy is produced by a stream turning a water wheel.

knead   to press, rub, or squeeze with the hands; massage.

> She *kneaded* the dough before shaping it into four loaves for baking.

lacerate   to tear jaggedly; mangle.

> The baby swallowed the safety pin, which caused an intestinal *laceration*.

laconic   brief or terse in speech or expression.

> His *laconic* replies conveyed much in few words.

languid   without interest or spirit; listless; indifferent.

> His *languid* walk irritated his companions, who were in a hurry.

languish   to lose vigor or vitality; fail in health; become weak; droop.

> He *languished* for weeks in miserable disappointment, refusing to leave the house or to see anybody.

lassitude   a state or feeling of being tired and listless; weariness; languor.

> The heat created a *lassitude* among the tourists that caused them to postpone their sightseeing.

latent   present but invisible or inactive; lying hidden and undeveloped within a person or thing, as a quality or power.

> He could see the *latent* possibilities of the situation.

laudable   praiseworthy; commendable.

> The girl listened to the old man's endless and repetitive stories with *laudable* patience.

laxity   looseness.

In summer, when business was slow, the manager allowed the employees some *laxity* in their hours.

legacy   anything handed down from, or as from, an ancestor.

He acquired the house as a *legacy* from his grandmother.

legible   that which can be read or deciphered.

Please print or type if your handwriting is not easily *legible.*

legislature   a body of persons given the responsibility and power to make laws for a country or state.

The federal *legislature* of the United States, the Congress, has two houses.

legitimate   sanctioned by law or custom; lawful.

The government of the country is *legitimate.*

lethargic   a condition of abnormal drowsiness or torpor.

The convalescent moved in a *lethargic* manner.

levity   lightness or gaiety of disposition, conduct, or speech.

The party toys and silly costumes epitomized the *levity* of the occasion.

liable   legally bound or obligated, as to make good any loss or damage that occurs in a transaction; responsible.

A physician is *liable* to contagion.

liaison   a linking up or connecting of the parts of a whole.

He had served as a *liaison* between the Allied command and the local government.

litigation   the act or process of carrying on a lawsuit.

As long as the estate is tied up in *litigation* by the would-be heirs, no one has use of the property.

longevity   long life, great span.

The Bible credits the first generations of men with a *longevity* unheard of today.

longitudinal of or in length.

> They measured the *longitudinal* distance carefully.

loquacious very talkative; fond of talking.

> A *loquacious* employee is a double time-waster; he invariably engages others as listeners.

lucid transparent.

> The directions were written in a style so *lucid* that a child could follow them.

lucrative producing wealth or profit; profitable; remunerative.

> A *lucrative* enterprise is attractive to investors.

Group 2

ludicrous laughably absurd.

> The play was intended to be *ludicrous*.

lugubrious very sad or mournful.

> The bloodhound had an endearingly *lugubrious* look.

macabre gruesome; grim and horrible; ghastly.

> The cannibals joined in a *macabre* dance around the boiling pot.

magisterial authoritative; official.

> One who is *magisterial* assumes the air of a master toward his pupils.

magnanimous noble-minded; high-souled.

> The painter was *magnanimous* enough to praise the work of a man he detested.

magnate a very important or influential person in any field of activity, esp. in a large business.

> The steel *magnate* refused to approve the consolidation.

magnitude of size.

> The apparent *magnitude* of the moon is greater near the horizon than at the zenith.

malfeasance   wrongdoing or misconduct, esp. by a public official.

> The governor was accused of acts of *malfeasance,* including taking graft.

malign   (adj.) showing ill will; malicious. (v.) to speak ill of.

> *Malign* comments are often motivated by jealousy.
> The students often *maligned* the strict professor.

malignant   wishing evil; very malevolent or malicious.

> A *malignant* person is dangerous, even as a friend.

malleable   that can be hammered, pounded, or pressed into various shapes without breaking; said of metals.

> Children are more *malleable* than adults and adapt to new environments more readily.

mandate   an authoritative order or command, esp. a written one.

> Some islands are still ruled by League of Nations or U.N. *mandate.*

manifest   to make clear or evident; show plainly; reveal; evince.

> He claims a greater devotion to that cause than his actions *manifest.*

mar   to injure or damage.

> The floor had been *marred* by scratches and scuff marks.

matriarch   a mother who rules her family or tribe.

> All important decisions were referred to the *matriarch* of the tribe.

matrix   that within which, as within and from which, something originates, takes form, or develops.

> The linotype machine is equipped with a brass *matrix* for each letter so that a line can be assembled and cast in lead.

maximum   the greatest quantity, number, or degree possible or permissable.

> In this course the *maximum* number of cuts allowed is six.

median   middle; intermediate.

> In a series of seven items, the fourth is the *median.*

mediocre   neither very good nor very bad; ordinary; average.

> A *mediocre* student in high school will rank low among candidates for college.

mellifluent   sounding sweet and smooth; honeyed.

> The soprano had an extremely *mellifluent* voice.

menace   projecting, threatening.

> The periodic floods *menaced* the city with destruction.

mendacious   not truthful; lying or false.

> Baron Munchausen was humorously *mendacious*.

meretricious   alluring by false, showy charms; attractive in a flashy way; tawdry.

> Her heavy makeup and the dim light combined to give her a *meretricious* allure.

meritorious   having merit; deserving reward.

> Medals were awarded for *meritorious* service.

metamorphose   to change in form or nature; transform.

> Two months abroad *metamorphosed* him into a man of the world.

Group 3

militate   to be directed; operate, or work against.

> A poor appearance at the interview will *militate* against your being hired.

minuscule   very small; tiny; minute.

> Such *minuscule* particles cannot be viewed with the usual classroom microscope.

minute   very small; tiny.

> The device records the presence of even *minute* amounts of radiation. The writer's *minute* attention to the refinements of style resulted in an elegantly worded essay.

misanthropy   hatred or distrust of all people.

The *misanthropy* of the hermit was known to all.

misappropriation   to appropriate to a bad, incorrect, or dishonest use.

The *misappropriation* of the funds caused much misery.

miscalculate   to calculate incorrectly; miscount or misjudge.

He failed because of his *miscalculations.*

miscellany   such a collection of writings, as in a book.

The old steamer trunk contained a *miscellany* of papers, clothes, and assorted junk.

miscreant   villainous; evil.

The *miscreant* kidnapper was caught and jailed.

misnomer   a wrong name or epithet applied to some person or thing.

At this season Muddy River is a *misnomer;* the waters are sweet and crystalline.

mitigate   make or become milder, less severe, less rigorous, or less painful.

He sought to *mitigate* the evil he had done.

mnemonics   a technique or system of improving the memory by the use of certain formulas.

Picture association is one of the keys to *mnemonics.*

mollify   to soothe the temper of; pacify; appease.

The irate customer was *mollified* by the manager's prompt action and apology.

morale   moral or mental condition with respect to courage, discipline, confidence, enthusiasm, or willingness to endure hardship, within a group.

After a landslide victory at the polls, *morale* in the party was at a peak.

morass   a tract of low, soft, watery ground; bog; marsh; swamp.

The application became mired in a *morass* of paperwork; there was no response for several weeks.

mordant biting, cutting, caustic, or sarcastic, as in speech, wit.

>His *mordant* remarks hurt her vanity.

mores ways that are considered conducive to the welfare of society and so, through general observance, develop the force of law, often becoming part of the formal legal code.

>The *mores* of any group are enforced by indoctrination and social pressure to conform.

moribund dying.

>The *moribund* king called for the prime minister.

morose ill-tempered; gloomy; sullen.

>The boy was *morose* for days over his failure to get tickets for the concert.

mundane of the world, esp. worldly, as distinguished from heavenly or spiritual.

>The film was undistinguished, a *mundane* exercise in horror movie clichés.

mutation a changing or being changed.

>He deplored the *mutations* of fortune.

mutilate to damage or otherwise make imperfect, esp. by removing an essential part of.

>The computer cannot read a *mutilated* card.

nauseate to cause nausea; to make sick.

>Food *nauseates* the patient.

nebulous cloudy; misty.

>He had a *nebulous* theory about memorizing key words as an aid to study.

negate make ineffective.

>The witness's full confession *negated* the need for further questions.

negative containing, expressing, or implying a denial or refusal.

>I received a *negative* answer to my request.

Group 4

negligible that which can be neglected or disregarded because small, unimportant, or trifling.

>The difference in their ages is *negligible*.

negotiate   to make arrangements for, settle, or conclude.

>   As long as both sides are willing to *negotiate* in good faith, a strike can be avoided.

neophyte   a new convert.

>   He gave lessons each night to the *neophytes.*

neurotic   characteristic of, or having a neurosis.

>   Hysterical pain—physical discomfort without organic cause—is a common *neurotic* symptom.

neutralize   to declare neutral in war.

>   The sea was *neutralized* by the nations through a treaty.

nihilism   the belief that there is no meaning or purpose in existence.

>   War fosters a spirit of *nihilism*, particularly among the defeated.

noctambulist   one who walks in his sleep.

>   The *noctambulist* had to be watched carefully.

nocturne   a romantic, dreamy musical composition, appropriate to night.

>   The *nocturne* was particularly dreamy and expressive.

nomenclature   the act or system of naming.

>   The *nomenclature* of botany had to be studied carefully.

nonagenarian   a person in his 90s.

>   The *nonagenarian* looks forward to a century mark.

nonchalant   showing cool lack of concern; casually indifferent.

>   The woman acted in a *nonchalant* manner, pretending not to notice the stars.

non sequitur   a remark having no bearing on what has just been said.

>   His speech was a tissue of *non sequiturs* that appealed to his audience's emotions at the expense of their intelligence.

novice   person new to a particular occupation or activity.

>   A *novice* in the job, she needed more time than an experienced worker to complete the same tasks.

noxious   harmful to the health; injurious.

>   The *noxious* fumes from the refinery poisoned the air.

nullify to make legally null; make void; annul.

> The new contract *nullifies* their previous agreement.

obdurate hardened and unrepenting; impenitent.

> He was *obdurate* and resisted the pleadings of his friends.

obeisance gesture of respect or reverence, such as bowing.

> They made an *obeisance* to the king.

obfuscate to muddle; confuse; bewilder.

> Do not *obfuscate* the facts with irrelevant issues.

objective (adv.) without bias or prejudice; detached; impersonal. (n.) aim, goal.

> It is extremely difficult to be *objective* about one's own weaknesses.
> Our *objective* is greater efficiency; we must study the possible means to that goal.

obliterate to do away with as if by effacing; destroy.

> The building had been completely *obliterated*.

oblivious causing forgetfulness.

> The absentminded professor was *oblivious* of the fire caused by his experiment.

obloquy ill repute, disgrace; or infamy resulting from this.

> He faced *obloquy* as a result of his ignoble actions.

obscure lacking light; dim; murky.

> His message was *obscure*.

obsequious much too willing to serve or obey; overly submissive; fawning.

> His *obsequious* obedience to the conquerors turned our stomachs.

obsess haunt or trouble the mind.

> He was *obsessed* with the idea he was important.

Group 5

obsolete no longer in use or practice.

> Since several offices have been relocated, the old directory is *obsolete*.

obstreperous noisy, boisterous or unruly, esp. in resisting or opposing.

> The *obstreperous* customer was asked to leave.

obtrude   to offer or force upon others unasked or unwanted.
>   It was unfair to *obtrude* upon their privacy.

obtuse   not sharp or pointed; blunt.
>   The man did not understand because of his *obtuse* wit.

obviate   to do away with or prevent by effective measures; make necessary.
>   *Obviate* the necessity for earning money, and all your time is your own.

occidental   a native of the Occident (western world), or a member of a people native to that region.
>   The finest gems come from *occidental* countries, according to some experts.

omnipotent   all-powerful.
>   By the end of the third match, he felt *omnipotent*.

onerous   burdensome; laborious.
>   His work was *onerous*.

onus   responsibility for a wrong; blame.
>   The *onus* of proof is on the accuser; the defendant is presumed innocent until proved guilty.

opprobrium   reproach; contempt for something regarded as inferior.
>   He deserved all the *opprobrium* he received for turning his back on a friend.

optimum   the best or most favorable degree, condition, amount, etc.
>   Under *optimum* conditions of light and moisture, the plant will grow to over three feet.

optional   left to one's option or choice; not compulsory; elective.
>   Air conditioning is *optional*; its cost is not included in the sticker price.

orbicular   in the form of an orb; spherical or circular.
>   The boomerang made an *orbicular* path back to the sender.

orifice   a mouth or aperture of a tube or cavity; opening.
>   The surgeon worked through an *orifice* below the ribs.

oscillate   to swing or move regularly back and forth.
>   The pendulum continued to *oscillate*, but the clock hands did not move.

ostensible   apparent; seeming or professed.
>   The *ostensible* purpose of the withdrawal was to pay a debt, but actually the money was used for entertainment.

ostentatious pretentious; showy.

Some people abhor large diamonds as being too *ostentatious*.

pacific of a peaceful nature or disposition; not warlike; mild; tranquil; calm.

The *Pacific* Ocean was so named by its discoverer because it was free from storms and tempests.

painstaking the act of taking great pains; great care or diligence.

The search for the lost ring was long and *painstaking*.

palliate to lessen the pain or severity of without actually curing; alleviate; ease.

He attempted to *palliate* his error by explaining the extenuating circumstances.

palpitate beat rapidly or flutter.

The *palpitation* of her heart was due to fright.

panacea a supposed remedy, cure, or medicine for all diseases or ills; cure-all.

Even money is no *panacea*.

panoramic a continuous series of scenes or events; a constantly changing scene.

From the summit of the mountain one has a *panoramic* view of the whole range.

pantheism the belief that God is not a personality but the sum of all beings, things, forces, etc. in the universe.

Monism is an essential element of *pantheism*.

pantoscopic affording a wide scope of vision, seeing everything.

Pantoscopic spectacles are spectacles that are divided into two segments, of which the upper is for distant vision and the lower is for reading or viewing near objects.

Group 6

paradigm a pattern, example or model to be copied.

The teacher handed out a sample letter as a *paradigm* of the correct form.

paradox a statement that seems contradictory, unbelievable.

"This sentence is false" is an example of a *paradox*.

paraphrase a rewording of the meaning expressed in something spoken or written.

To *paraphrase* someone's work without acknowledging the source of one's information is a form of plagiarism.

parity   the state or condition of being the same in power, value or rank.

Congress aims to keep farm prices at 80 percent of a *parity* with prices of manufactured goods.

parsimonious   misery; close.

Although she lived in prosperous comfort, she seemed *parsimonious* to her more extravagant relatives.

partisan   a person who takes the part of or strongly supports one side, party, or person.

Partisan loyalty can no longer be taken for granted; voters are now attracted to individuals more than to parties.

patent   (adj.) obvious; plain; evident. (n.) exclusive right, as to a product or invention.

The promise of tax relief was a *patent* attempt to win last-minute support from the farmers.

The company's *patent* on the formula expires after a certain number of years.

patron   a person, usually a wealthy and influential one, who sponsors and supports some person, activity, or institution.

For donating her time and energy to the museum, she was honored as a *patron* of the arts.

peccadillo   minor or petty sin; slight fault.

He insisted on caviling over *peccadillos.*

pecuniary   of or involving money.

He had no *pecuniary* interest in the project.

pedantic   unnecessary stress on minor or trivial points of learning, displaying a scholarship lacking in judgment or sense of proportion.

The *pedantic* pedagogue pedaled to the palace spouting Platonic principles.

penchant   to incline.

He has a *penchant* for making friends.

pending   not decided, determined, or established.

It required much patience to wait while the petition was *pending.*

penurious   unwilling to part with money or possessions; mean; miserly; stingy.

A poor man is *penurious* by necessity.

perambulate   to walk through, over, around.

We *perambulated* over the grounds for several hours.

perceive to grasp mentally; make note of.

I *perceived* that the beast was harmless.

perception the act of perceiving or the ability to perceive; mental grasp of objects.

Perception is that act of the mind whereby the mind becomes conscious of anything, including hunger, thirst, cold, or heat.

percussion the hitting or impact of one body against another.

The drum is a *percussion* instrument.

peremptory that which cannot be denied, changed, delayed, or opposed.

The captain gave a *peremptory* command for a major advance.

peripheral of belonging to, or forming a boundary line or perimeter; outer; external; merely incidental.

The man who notices people almost behind him has excellent *peripheral* vision.

permeable open to passage or penetration, esp. by fluids.

Most clay dishes are *permeable*.

permutation any radical alteration; total transformation.

The sequences CBA and BCA are *permutations* of ABC.

pernicious causing great injury; destruction.

Excessive drinking is a *pernicious* habit.

perpendicular at right angles to a given plane or line.

The lamppost, having been grazed by the truck, was no longer *perpendicular*.

perpetrate to do or perform; be guilty of.

The committee *perpetrated* the hoax in an attempt to defame the rival candidate.

Group 7

persist to refuse to give up, esp. when faced with opposition or difficulty; continue firmly or steadily.

Despite the rebuffs, he *persisted* in his efforts to befriend the disturbed youngster.

perspicuity easily understood; lucid.

His *perspicuity* made him an excellent teacher.

peruse   to read carefully, or thoroughly; study.

> She *perused* the text, absorbing as much information as she could.

pervious   allowing passage through; that which can be penetrated or permeated.

> The man was *pervious* to criticism and often benefited from the constructive advice of his colleagues.

petulance   impatient or irritable, esp. over a petty annoyance; peevish.

> *Petulance* is a vestige of childhood desire for more parental attention.

placate   to stop from being angry; appease; pacify; mollify.

> A quick temper is often easily *placated.*

placid   undisturbed; tranquil; calm; quiet.

> The drug had relieved her anxiety, leaving her in a *placid* and jovial mood.

polemics   the art or practice of disputation or controversy.

> He is an expert at *polemics* and is studying for a career in law.

pontificate   to speak or act in a pompous or dogmatic way.

> He would rise slowly, *pontificate* for half an hour, and sit down without having said a thing we didn't know before.

portentous   ominous; arousing awe or amazement; marvelous; prodigious.

> The thunderstorm that broke as we were leaving seemed *portentous,* but in fact the weather was lovely for the rest of the trip.

posterity   all succeeding generations; future mankind.

> Many things we build today are for *posterity.*

potential   that can, but has not yet, come into being.

> If she qualifies for the promotion, her *potential* earnings for the next year might be close to $20,000.

precarious   dependent upon chance; risky.

> His position on the ledge was *precarious.*

precedent   an act, statement, legal decision, case, etc. that may serve as an example, reason, or justification for a later one.

> The lawyer's brief argued that the legal *precedents* cited by the opposition were not relevant because of subsequent changes in the law.

precipitous   steep like a precipice.

> The road had a *precipitous* drop on the south side.

precise   strictly defined; accurately stated; definite.

> The coroner determined the *precise* time of murder by examining the victim.

preclude   make impossible.

> Obeying the law would *preclude* my getting home in five minutes.

precocious   developed or matured to a point beyond that which is normal for the age.

> *Precocious* children should be given enriched programs of study.

precursor   a person or thing that goes before; forerunner; harbinger.

> The Continental Congress was the *precursor* of our bicameral Congress of today.

predecessor   a person who precedes or preceded another, as in office.

> In his inaugural address the new president of the association praised the work done by his *predecessor*.

predicament   a condition or situation, now specif. one that is difficult, unpleasant, or embarrassing.

> Having promised to balance the budget, to cut taxes, and to increase defense spending, the newly-elected president found himself in a hopeless *predicament*.

predilection   a preconceived liking, partiality, or preference.

> He had a *predilection* for good food at any price.

predominantly   most frequent; noticeable.

> Although there are a few older students, the class is *predominantly* made up of eighteen-year-olds.

prejudiced   a judgment or opinion formed before the facts are known.

> Since I have never liked westerns, I was *prejudiced* against the film before I ever saw it.

premeditation   a degree of planning and forethought sufficient to show intent to commit an act.

> The *premeditation* of the crime was what made it so heinous.

Group 8

preoccupied   previously or already occupied.

Preoccupied by her dilemma, she missed her stop on the train.

prerogative   a prior or exclusive right or privilege.

Going home after school is your *prerogative*.

prescribe   to give medical advice or prescriptions.

For the headache the physician *prescribed* aspirin.

presume   to take upon oneself without permission or authority; dare; venture.

I was furious that she had *presumed* to take the car without permission.

prevaricate   to turn aside from; evade the truth.

When questioned directly, the suspect was forced to *prevaricate*.

primordial   first in time; existing at or from the beginning.

The *primordial* world had no human beings.

principal   first in rank, authority, importance, degree.

The *principal* city economically is also the most populous in the state.

principle   a fundamental truth, law, doctrine, or motivating force.

A man of *principle* never goes back on his word.

probity   uprightness in one's dealings; complete honesty; integrity.

The *probity* of the witness was placed in doubt.

proceed   to advance or go on, esp. after stopping.

Because of numerous interruptions, the work *proceeded* slowly.

proclaim   to announce officially; announce to be.

When the victory was announced, a holiday was *proclaimed* and all work ground to a halt.

proclivity   a natural or habitual tendency or inclination.

He had a *proclivity* for getting into trouble.

procure   to get or bring about by some effort; obtain; secure.

At the last minute the convict's attorney *procured* a stay of execution.

prodigious of great size, power, extent.

He had a *prodigious* nose and a tiny mouth.

profligate immoral and shameless; dissolute.

The *profligate* son was a regular source of income for his father's attorney.

prolong to lengthen or extend in time or space.

The treatment *prolongs* life but cannot cure the disease, which is terminal.

propinquity nearness in time or place.

The *propinquity* of gas stations decreased the value of the property.

proscribe to deprive of the protection of the law; outlaw.

Theft is *proscribed* mostly by state law.

prospectus a statement outlining the main features of a new work or business enterprise, or the attractions of an established institution such as a college or hotel.

The *prospectus* for the real estate development was mailed to potential investors.

protagonist the main character in a drama, novel, or story, around whom the action centers.

Mike Hammer is the *protagonist* of a whole series of detective stories.

protocol the code of ceremonial forms and courtesies accepted as proper and correct in official dealings, as between heads of states or diplomatic officials.

Protocol demands that we introduce the ambassador before the special envoy; to fail to do so would be interpreted as an affront.

prototype the first thing or being of its kind; model; archetype.

Homer's *Iliad* became the *prototype* for much of the later epic poetry of Europe.

protract to draw out; lengthen in duration; prolong.

The jury's deliberations were *protracted* by confusion over a point of law.

protuberance projection; bulge; swelling.

Jimmy Durante was proud of his facial *protuberance*.

provocation an act or instance of provoking; esp. a cause of resentment or irritation; incitement.

The attack, coming without *provocation*, took them by surprise.

Challenge 64

Choose the word or phrase that means most nearly the same as the key word or the italicized word.

1. lethargic
   a. romantic
   b. sluggish
   c. oily
   d. melodic

2. peccadillo
   a. wild pig
   b. burrowing mam-
   c. mal
   d. petty fault
      bric-a-brac

3. mitigate
   a. lessen
   b. incite
   c. measure
   d. prosecute

4. nebulous
   a. cloudy
   b. subdued
   c. awkward
   d. careless

5. laudable
   a. arrogant
   b. clean
   c. boisterous
   d. praiseworthy

6. legible
   a. printed
   b. allowed
   c. typed
   d. readable

7. levity
   a. mediterranean
   b. floatable
   c. frivolity
   d. illumination

8. malign
   a. defame
   b. break
   c. separate
   d. injure

9. loquacious
   a. birdlike
   b. winding
   c. rich
   d. talkative

10. mendacious
    a. beggared
    b. dishonest
    c. intelligent
    d. laudable

11. miscreant
    a. aborted
    b. deformed
    c. villainous
    d. mistaken

12. nonchalant
    a. unattainable
    b. excitable
    c. nonessential
    d. indifferent

13. He was asked to *pacify* the visitor. The word *pacify* means most nearly
    a. escort
    b. interview
    c. calm
    d. detain

14. magnanimous
    a. insolent
    b. shrewd
    c. unselfish
    d. threatening

15. morose
    a. curious
    b. gloomy
    c. impatient
    d. timid

Challenge 65

Choose the word or phrase that is most nearly opposite in meaning to the given word.

1. polemic
   a. arctic
   b. electrochemical
   c. agreeable
   d. statistical

2. laconic
   a. watery
   b. musical
   c. vivacious
   d. verbose

3. languid
   a. fluent
   b. moist
   c. sickly
   d. vigorous

4. lassitude
   a. tangle
   b. long-winded-ness
   c. determination
   d. vitality

5. latent
   a. obvious
   b. invented
   c. troubled
   d. unique

6. obfuscate
   a. lame
   b. placate
   c. adulterate
   d. clarify

7. obviate
   a. grasp
   b. reform
   c. make necessary
   d. smooth

8. petulant
   a. irascible
   b. cheerful
   c. uncouth
   d. abnormal

9. objective
   a. biased
   b. personal
   c. aimless
   d. eastern

10. obsequious
    a. respectful
    b. bold
    c. hereditary
    d. murky

11. placate
    a. amuse
    b. antagonize
    c. embroil
    d. pity

12. lucrative
    a. debasing
    b. unprofitable
    c. influential
    d. monetary

13. ostensible
    a. showy
    b. unintelligible
    c. rust-free
    d. blended

14. mollify
    a. fortify
    b. lullaby
    c. shame
    d. intensify

15. parsimony
    a. contradiction
    b. prodigality
    c. clinch
    d. penury

Module 5: *Proximity–Zenith*

Group 1

proximity   the state or quality of being near; nearness in space or time.

> The *proximity* of the shopping mall is a great advantage to those residents who do not drive.

psychic   of or having to do with the psyche or mind.

> He claimed special *psychic* powers, including the ability to foresee the future.

punctilious   very careful about every detail of behavior or ceremony.

> Be *punctilious* in obeying your doctor.

punctuality   carefully observant of an appointed time; on time; prompt.

> The train had an excellent record for *punctuality*; it almost always arrived precisely at 8:15.

pusillanimous   timid, cowardly, or irresolute; faint-hearted.

> A young *pusillanimous* infantryman is a danger to an entire company.

putative   generally considered or deemed such; reputed.

> His *putative* wealth was exaggerated by his ostentation.

quadrennial   lasting four years; occurring once every four years.

> The *quadrennial* games were anticipated eagerly.

quandary   doubt, uncertainty, a state of difficulty or perplexity.

> He was in a *quandary* because the problem was so complex.

query   to question (a person).

> He *queried* the witness about his alibi.

quiescent   to become quiet.

> The eternal problem of juvenile delinquency becomes *quiescent* during the excitement of war.

quintessence   the pure, concentrated essence of anything.

> It is the *quintessence* of coffee flavor.

quixotic   extravagantly chivalrous or romantically idealistic.

> His actions were *quixotic* and thoroughly useless.

quorum   the minimum number of members that must be present for an assembly to conduct business.

> No votes may be taken until there are enough representatives present to constitute a *quorum.*

quota   a share or proportion which each of a number is called upon to contribute, or which is assigned to each; proportional share.

> The school had an unwritten *quota* system that set limits on the proportion of applicants from different geographical areas.

quote   to reproduce or repeat a passage from or a statement of.

> He *quoted* the words of Woodrow Wilson in his speech.

quotidian   daily; recurring every day.

> He had a *quotidian* fever.

radiation   the act or process of sending out rays of heat, light, etc.

> Solar *radiation* is the *radiation* of the sun as estimated by the amount of energy that reaches the earth.

ramification   a branch or offshoot.

> The *ramifications* of the subject were complex.

rampant   spreading unchecked; widespread; rife.

> The *rampant* growth of weeds made the lawn look extremely unsightly.

rancor   a continuing and bitter hate or ill will; deep spite or malice.

> In spite of the insults of his opponent, the man remained calm and spoke without *rancor.*

rapidity   speed.

> The *rapidity* with which her hands flew over the piano keys was too great to follow with the eye.

ratio   fixed relation in degree or number.

> The *ratio* of women to men in middle-level positions in the firm is only one to seven.

rationale   the fundamental reasons, or rational basis for something.

> They defended their discrimination with the *rationale* that women were incompetent physically to handle the job.

reactionary   of, characterized by, or advocating reaction, esp. in politics.

> The pamphlet expressed a *reactionary* hatred of innovation and nostalgia for "the good old days."

rebuke   to blame or scold in a sharp way; reprimand.

He *rebuked* the puppy in stern tones for chewing the carpet.

Group 2

rebuttal   contradiction, reply to a charge or argument.

Each side was allowed five minutes for *rebuttal* of the other side's arguments.

recalcitrant   refusing to obey authority; stubborn.

A *recalcitrant* child is a difficult pupil.

recapitulate   to repeat briefly, as in an outline; summarize.

It is not my purpose to *recapitulate* all the topics that should find a place in democracy's message to the people.

recede   to go or move back.

The waters *receded* and left the beach covered with seaweed.

receptive   receiving or tending to receive; take in, admit, or contain.

The manager, unsatisfied with the store's appearance, was *receptive* to the idea of a major remodeling.

recessive   receding or tending to recede.

The characteristic encoded in a *recessive* gene may be passed on to an individual's offspring even though it is not apparent in the individual.

recipient   a person or thing that receives.

The *recipient* of the award had been chosen from among 200 candidates.

recollect   to call back to mind.

He could not *recollect* having made the appointment.

reconcile   to make friendly again or win over to a friendly attitude; bring into harmony.

After hours of recalculating the incorrect figures, we were able to *reconcile* the two accounts.

recourse   that to which one turns when seeking aid or safety.

Unless you correct this error immediately, I will have no *recourse* but to complain to the manager.

recriminate   to answer an accuser by accusing him in return.

They *recriminated* constantly over the most trivial setbacks, each blaming the other whenever anything went wrong.

rectitude   conduct according to moral principles; strict honesty; uprightness of character.

> Her unfailing *rectitude* in business dealings made her well trusted among her associates.

recur   to have recourse (to); to return, as in thought, talk, or memory; to occur again as in talk or memory.

> Unless social conditions are improved, the riots are bound to *recur*.

redeem   to buy back; to get back; justify.

> Though the film is boring in parts, it is *redeemed* by a gripping finale.

redress   compensation or satisfaction, as for a wrong done.

> The petitioners asked the state for a *redress* of grievances for which they had no legal recourse.

refrain   to hold back; forbear; curb.

> Considerate parents *refrain* from criticizing their children in front of others.

reiterate   to say or do again, repeat.

> The instructions were *reiterated* before each new section of the test.

relegate   to exile or banish; to consign or assign to an inferior position.

> He *relegated* the policeman to a suburban beat.

remit   to forgive or pardon; to send in payment.

> The invoice was *remitted* by check; you should be receiving it shortly.

renege   to back out of an agreement; to go back on a promise.

> Their assurances of good faith were hollow; they *reneged* on the agreement almost at once.

renounce   to give up; cast off or disown; repudiate.

> The nation was urged to *renounce* its dependence on imports and to buy more American cars.

reprehend   to reprimand or rebuke.

> He was *reprehended* for his rudeness and sent to his room.

repress   to keep down or hold back; restrain; subdue.

> We could not *repress* a certain nervousness as the plane bumped along the runway.

reprimand   a severe or formal rebuke by someone in authority.

> Since it was a first offense, the judge let the teenager off with a *reprimand*.

reprove   to express disapproval of; censure.

The instructor *reproved* the student for failing to hand in the assignments on time.

Group 3

repudiate   to refuse to have anything to do with.

The candidate *repudiated* the endorsement of the Communist party.

rescind   to revoke, repeal, or cancel.

They *rescinded* their offer of aid when they became disillusioned with the project.

restitution   a giving back to a rightful owner of something that has been lost or taken away; restoration.

He agreed to make *restitution* for the money he had stolen.

retain   to hold or keep in possession.

Throughout the grueling day she had managed somehow to *retain* her sense of humor.

reticent   to have a restrained, quiet, or understated quality.

His *reticence* kept him from offering answers.

retroactive   going into effect as of a specified date in the past.

A law may not apply *retroactively*.

retrogress   to go or move backward.

Because of the devastation of the recent earthquakes, living conditions in the region have *retrogressed*.

revive   to come or bring back to life or consciousness.

A cool drink and a bath *revived* her spirits.

risibility   a sense of the ridiculous or amusing; appreciation of what is laughable.

His *risibility* increased with each act of the play.

rupture   the act of breaking off or bursting; the state of being broken apart or burst.

The bungling of the rescue operation, which resulted in the death of the ambassador, led to a *rupture* of diplomatic relations between the two nations.

sagacious   having or showing keen perception or discernment and sound judgment and foresight.

> Teachers have more *sagacity* than students give them credit for.

salient   standing out from the rest; conspicuous; noticeable; prominent.

> The *salient* points of the speech could not be forgotten by the audience.

sanctimony   affected piety or righteousness; religious hypocrisy.

> His *sanctimony* served to hide the fact that he indulged in the very vices he publicly condemned.

sanction   authorized approval or permission.

> The parent organization refused to *sanction* the illegal demonstration stated by the splinter group.

sardonic   disdainfully or bitterly sneering; ironical or sarcastic.

> His *sardonic* smile irritated the guests.

satiate   to satisfy to the full.

> Employees at candy factories soon get so *satiated* that they never eat the stuff.

schism   a split or division in an organized group or society, esp. a church as the result of difference of opinion or doctrine.

> The Great *Schism* created two Christian churches, the Eastern and the Western.

secular   not sacred or religious.

> The *secular* authorities often have differences with the church in Italy.

secure   (adj.) free from fear, care, doubt, or anxiety. (v.) to make safe, to obtain.

> Her *secure* job assured her of a steady income for as long as she chose to work.
> I have *secured* two tickets for tonight's performance.

sedulous   working hard and steadily; diligent.

> He was a *sedulous* worker.

sentient   to perceive by the senses.

> Even a dog is *sentient*.

sequester   to set off or apart; separate; segregate.

> The jury was *sequestered* until the members could reach a verdict.

simulate   to give a false indication or appearance of; pretend; feign.

Although she had guessed what the gift would be, she *simulated* surprise when she unwrapped the package.

simultaneous   occurring or existing at the same time.

There were *simultaneous* broadcasts of the game on local television and radio stations.

solicitude   care, concern, etc.; sometimes, excessive care or concern.

The teacher had a great *solicitude* for the welfare of her students.

Group 4

somatic   of the body, as distinguished from the soul.

Psychological disturbances often result in *somatic* symptoms.

sonorous   producing or capable of producing sound, esp. sound of full, deep, or rich quality.

His *sonorous* voice helped make him a famous orator.

soporific   tending to or causing sleep.

Because of the drug's *soporific* effect, you should not try to drive after taking it.

specious   plausible but not genuine.

He advanced his cause with *specious* arguments.

spurious   not true or genuine; false; counterfeit.

The junta's promise of free elections was *spurious*, a mere sop to world opinion.

stentorian   very loud.

His *stentorian* voice carried across the auditorium without aid.

stoical   showing austere indifference to joy, grief, pleasure, or pain.

He was *stoical* in the face of great misfortunes.

stratagem   a trick, scheme, or plan for deceiving an enemy in war.

He presented another *stratagem* to overcome the lead of the opposition.

strident   harsh-sounding; shrill; grating.

She had a *strident* voice that sent shivers down my back.

stringent   severe, strict, compelling.

The speaker presented *stringent* arguments for the unwelcome cutbacks.

subcutaneous   being used or introduced beneath the skin.

Injections of most vaccines are *subcutaneous*.

subdue   conquer; vanquish; reduce; diminish; soften.

The understanding actions of the nurse helped to *subdue* the stubborn and unruly child.

submit   to yield to the action, control, or power of another or others.

Although the doctors were dubious of his full recovery, the patient refused to *submit* to despair.
The couple *submitted* their application to the loan officer.

subpoena   a written legal order directing a person to appear in court to give testimony, show specified records, etc.

They issued *subpoenas* to all necessary witnesses.

subterfuge   any plan, action, or device used to hide one's true objective.

The lie about a previous engagement was a *subterfuge* by which they avoided a distasteful duty.

subversive   tending or seeking to subvert, overthrow, or destroy.

The editor was accused of disseminating propaganda *subversive* to the national security.

successor   a person or thing that succeeds or follows another.

Retiring from office, the mayor left a budget crisis and a transit strike to his *successor*.

suffuse   to overspread so as to fill with a glow, color, or fluid.

The floor was *suffused* with a disinfectant wax.

supercilious   disdainful or contemptuous.

The *supercilious* attitude of wealthy families has been a cause of many social upheavals.

superfluous   being more than is needed, useful, or wanted; surplus.

It was clear from the scene what had happened; his lengthy explanations were *superfluous*.

supersede   to take the place of in office, function, or responsibility; succeed.

The administration appointed new department heads to *supersede* the old.

supervise   to oversee; direct; manage.

> A new employee must be carefully *supervised* to insure that he learns the routine correctly and thoroughly.

supplicate   to ask for earnestly and humbly, as by prayer.

> He *supplicated* for a pardon.

surfeit   excess.

> There was a *surfeit* of food at the table, and no one could finish the meal.

surreptitious   acting in a secret, stealthy way.

> They met *surreptitiously* in the night to exchange information.

Group 5

suspend   to cease or cause to become inoperative for a time; stop temporarily; to hang by a support from above so as to allow free movement.

> Service on the line was *suspended* while the tracks were being repaired. The light fixture was *suspended* from the beam by a chain.

symposium   any meeting or social gathering at which ideas are freely exchanged.

> They listened to a television *symposium* on the subject of better schools.

synthesis   the putting together of parts or elements so as to form a whole.

> Photo*synthesis* is the process of making plant food from air and water, with the aid of sunlight.

tacitly   making no sound; unspoken; not expressed or declared openly, but implied or understood.

> He *tacitly* assented to the arguments of his wife.

tangential   going off at a tangent; diverging or digressing.

> Facts about the author's life, while they may be fascinating, are *tangential* to an evaluation of her works.

tangible   that which can be touched or felt by touch; having actual form and substance.

> The new position offered an opporutnity for creativity as well as the more *tangible* reward of a higher salary.

tardiness   behind time; late, delayed, or dilatory.

> His *tardiness* was habitual; he was late getting to class most mornings.

tedious   boring, long or verbose; wearisome; tiresome.

The film was so *tedious* that we walked out in disgust before it was half over.

temporize   to suit one's actions to the time, occasion, or circumstances, without reference to principle.

He *temporized* until he knew what they wanted from him.

tenable   that which can be held, defended, or maintained.

The club had no *tenable* reasons for the exclusion; it was purely a case of prejudice.

tenacity   perserverance; firmness; retentiveness.

His *tenacity* as an investigator earned him the nickname "Bulldog."

tenuous   not substantial; slight or flimsy.

The business survived on a *tenuous* relationship with one customer.

terminate   to bring to an end in space or time.

She *terminated* the interview by standing up and thanking us for coming.

terse   free of superfluous words.

The official's *terse* replies to our questions indicated that he did not welcome being interrupted.

thesaurus   a treasury or storehouse; a book of synonyms and antonyms.

A good *thesaurus* distinguishes the shades of meaning among words with similar definitions.

thesis   an unproved statement assumed as a premise.

He completed his doctoral *thesis*.

torpidity   slow and dull; apathetic.

His *torpidity* mounted to a total loss of sensation.

tractable   easily managed.

A *tractable* worker is a boon to the supervisor but is not always a good leader.

traduce   to say untrue or malicious things about.

Her reputation was *traduced* by malicious innuendo.

transcendent   beyond the limits of possible experience.

The high cost of the house was due to its obviously *transcendent* worth.

transcribe   to write out or type out in full.

> These almost illegible notes must be *transcribed* before anyone else will be able to use them.

transcript   something made by or based on transcribed, written, typewritten, or printed copy.

> The court reporter read from the *transcript* of the witness's testimony.

transgression   the act or an instance of transgressing; breach of a law or duty.

> We ask God to forgive our *transgressions*.

transitory   adapted for passing through.

> It is normal to feel a *transitory* depression over life's setbacks.

translate   to change from one place, position, or condition to another.

> The flight attendant *translated* the announcement into Spanish for the benefit of two of the passengers.

Group 6

transmute   change from one form, species, condition, nature, or substance to another.

> Water power can be *transmuted* into electricity.

transverse   to pass, move, or extend over, across, or through; across.

> They placed the ties *transversely* on the tracks and waited for the train to crash.

trenchant   keen, penetrating, incisive.

> His *trenchant* remarks were more dangerous than his sword.

trepidation   trembling movement; quaking; fearful uncertainty; anxiety; apprehension.

> The stories they had heard caused them much *trepidation*.

tribulation   great misery or distress, as from oppression; deep sorrow.

> The Pilgrims faced many *tribulations* before the first colonies were firmly established.

truculent   fierce, cruel, or savage, esp. of speech or writing.

> The champion's *truculent* manner intimidated the challenger.

truncate   to shorten by cutting.

> The shrubs were uniformly *truncated* to form a neat hedge.

turbulent   full of commotion or wild disorder; unruly or boisterous.
The *turbulent* stream claimed many lives.

turgid   swollen; distended.
The man was in constant pain because his limbs were *turgid* as the result of an incurable disease.

turpitude   baseness; vileness; depravity.
A person convicted of moral *turpitude* may not be permitted entry into the United States.

ubiquity   seeming to be everywhere at the same time; omnipresence.
The *ubiquity* of God has often been denied.

ultimately   as a final result; at last.
Afflictions may *ultimately* prove to be blessings.

umbrage   shade; shadow; offense or resentment.
He takes *umbrage* if you look at him sideways.

uncanny   mysterious or unfamiliar; strange; eerie; weird.
After a lifetime of fishing those waters, the old man was able to predict weather changes with *uncanny* precision.

uncouth   awkward; clumsy; unrefined.
His *uncouth* behavior was marked by a simple inability to handle a knife and fork.

undulating   moving in or as in waves; moving sinuously.
A stretch of country is said to be *undulating* when it presents a succession of elevations and depressions resembling waves of the sea.

unethical   without or not according to moral principles.
Although he did not break any law, the man's conduct in taking advantage of credulous clients was certainly *unethical*.

uniform   always the same; not varying in degree or rate; consistent at all times.
Most countries do not have a *uniform* temperature.

unilateral   involving or obligating only one of several persons or parties; not reciprocal.
A *unilateral* bond is one that binds one party only.

unmitigated   not lessened or eased.
According to President Eliot of Harvard, inherited wealth is an *unmitigated* curse when divorced from culture.

unprecedented   having no precedent or parallel; unheard-of; novel.
>   Sputnik 1 accomplished *unprecedented* feats.

unscrupulous   unprincipled; not constrained by ideas of right and wrong.
>   The *unscrupulous* landlord refused to return the security deposit, claiming falsely that the tenant had damaged the apartment.

unwieldy   hard to wield, manage, handle, or deal with because of large size or weight, or awkward form.
>   Four men were required to move the *unwieldy* rock.

upbraid   to rebuke severely or bitterly; censure sharply.
>   The husband *upbraided* his wife for her extravagances.

urbane   polite and courteous in a smooth, polished way; refined.
>   He travels in *urbane* circles and is as suave as any of his friends.

Group 7

usurpation   the act of usurping; esp., the unlawful or violent seizure of a throne, government, or power.
>   The *usurpation* of the kingdom by the conquerors caused much misery.

uxorious   excessively or foolishly fond of or submissive to one's wife.
>   He was described as an *uxorious* husband.

vacate   to leave empty.
>   The court ordered the demonstrators to *vacate* the premises.

vacillation   fluctuation of mind; unsteadiness of character; change from one purpose to another; inconstancy.
>   His *vacillation* in giving orders made him difficult to work for.

vacuous   empty; having or showing lack of intelligence, interest, or thought; stupid; senseless; inane.
>   His *vacuous* speeches won him no converts.

vain   worthless; futile; unprofitable; conceited.
>   They tried in *vain* to win the game.

vanquish   to conquer; overcome; overpower; force into submission.
>   Napoleon *vanquished* the Austrian army.

vapid   tasteless, flavorless or flat; uninteresting, dull, or boring.
>   The time was passed in *vapid* conversation about the weather.

variable   changeable, fluctuating, or varied.
>   The weather report stated that the winds would be *variable.*

variegate   to make varied in appearance by differences; diversify.
>   The builder created a *variegated* pattern with marble of different hues.

verbatim   word for word; in exactly the same words.
>   The lawyer requested the defendant to repeat the speech *verbatim.*

verbose   using more words than are necessary; wordy; long-winded; prolix.
>   The audience was bored by the *verbose* politician.

verdict   decision, esp. a legal judgment of guilt or innocence.
>   The *verdict* of a jury in convicting a defendant must be unanimous.

verify   to prove to be true by demonstration, evidence, or testimony.
>   The principal expected the student to *verify* his statements.

verisimilitude   the appearance of being true and real.
>   There is a great *verisimilitude* here, but I still do not believe this is conclusive evidence.

verity   truthfulness; honesty; reality.
>   The *verity* of the document could not be questioned.

vernacular   using the native language of a country or place.
>   He spoke in the *vernacular* of southern Germany.

vertex   top; highest point; apex; zenith.
>   The view was breathtaking from the *vertex* of the hill.

vestige   a trace, mark or sign of something that once existed but has passed away or disappeared.
>   The artifacts were the last *vestiges* of an earlier civilization.

viability   the capacity to live and continue normal development.
>   The statistician compiled a chart that indicated the *viability* of male infants as compared with that of female infants.

vicarious   shared in or experienced by imagined participation in another's experience.
>   She took a *vicarious* pleasure in the achievements of her daughter.

vicissitude   unpredictable changes or variations that keep occurring in life, fortune, etc.; shifting circumstances; up and downs.
>   The *vicissitude* of fortune made him a poor man.

vigilant   staying watchful and alert to danger or trouble.
As a Supreme Court Justice he had always been *vigilant* against any attempt to encroach on the freedoms guaranteed by the Bill of Rights.

vilify   to use abusive or slanderous language about or of; calumniate; revile; defame.
He was sued for attempting to *vilify* the physician.

vindicate   to clear from criticism, blame, or guilt.
The judgment of the author was *vindicated* by the success of the text.

Group 8

vindictive   unforgiving; revengeful.
Stung by the negative reviews of his film, the director made *vindictive* personal remarks about critics.

vitality   power to live; to endure or survive.
She had been physically active all her life and at the age of eighty still possessed great *vitality*.

vociferous   loud, noisy, or vehement in making one's feelings known; clamorous.
There are some who come to meetings merely to add to the *vociferous* din.

volatile   likely to shift quickly and unpredictably; unstable; explosive.
She had a *volatile* temper—easily angered and easily appeased.

volition   the act of using the will; conscious and deliberate decision.
He performed the act of his own *volition*.

waive   to give up or forego a right, claim, or privilege.
In cases of unusual hardship, the normal fee may be *waived*.

warp   to distort; twist; bend slightly.
The board *warped* in the sun.
His ideas were *warped* by a bad environment.

warrant   to serve as justification or reasonable grounds for.
The infraction was too minor to *warrant* a formal reprimand.

wayward   headstrong; wilful; disobedient.
The *wayward* flight of the bat was difficult to trace.

weld   to unite (pieces of metal, etc.) by heating; to unite into a single whole.
Steel bars were *welded* to make a frame.

welter   to roll about or wallow.
He took the *welter* of the crowds in stride, slipping down the street as quickly as he could.

wheedle   to influence a person by flattery, soothing words, or coaxing.
>   The woman knew exactly how to *wheedle* what she wanted from the man.

wield   to handle, use, and control.
>   The soldier was skilled at *wielding* his sword.

wily   crafty; sly; artful; cunning.
>   He was *wily* enough to avoid detection.

wince   to shrink, as from a blow or from pain; flinch.
>   He *winced* under her sarcasm.

winnow   to examine, sift for the purpose of separating the bad from the good.
>   His statement was so garbled that it was impossible to *winnow* the falsehoods from the truth.

wont   usual practice, habit, or custom.
>   He was *wont* to stroll about the grounds before breakfast.

wraith   a ghost.
>   When the children entered the haunted house, they fully expected to encounter *wraiths.*

wrest   to take by violence; to usurp, extort, or wring.
>   It was impossible for the child to *wrest* his toy from the bigger boy.

wry   produced by distortion of features.
>   He made a *wry* face when I suggested castor oil.

xenophobia   fear and hatred of strangers or foreigners.
>   The *xenophobia* of the candidate expressed itself in his extreme and unrealistic isolationism.

yearn   to be filled with longing or desire.
>   The parents *yearned* for their recently deceased child.

yowl   a protracted, wailing cry.
>   The dog's *yowls* went on all night.

zeal   ardor; fervor; intense enthusiasm; earnestness.
>   He left a record for *zeal* that cannot fail to be an inspiration.

zenith   point directly overhead; the highest point; peak.
>   The sun reaches its *zenith* at noon.

Challenge 66

Select the word or phrase that will best complete the meaning of the sentence as a whole.

1. Her comments were so _____ that we couldn't remember the real point of the discussion.
   a. crude
   b. informative
   c. unfriendly
   d. wavering
   e. tangential

2. A news reporter, committed to printing only that which is true, always _____ a story before deadline.
   a. verbifies
   b. verifies
   c. ascertains
   d. villifies
   e. violates

3. Because she prided herself on being of strong will, she quit smoking through her own , not because she was forced to.
   a. malice
   b. volition
   c. paranoia
   d. vocation
   e. avocation

4. There was a _____ of gold-leafing on the mirror which made it look gaudy.
   a. facade
   b. quantity
   c. depression
   d. surfeit
   e. surface

5. Matters pertaining to daily life are referred to as _____ as opposed to religious.
   a. sectarian
   b. secluded
   c. secular
   d. secretive
   e. secondary

6. In some communist countries, residents are jailed as _____ when authorities feel that they are trying to overthrow the government.
   a. incurables
   b. incorrigibles
   c. perversives
   d. subversives
   e. reversives

7. Our understanding of the finances involved was so _____ that we needed outside advice.
   a. tenuous
   b. tenant
   c. astute
   d. sure
   e. worried

8. The potion contained a powerful substance that caused _____ and allowed the enemy to walk past undisturbed.
   a. rapidity
   b. torpidity
   c. arrogance
   d. hesitance
   e. obesity

9. The speaker's points were so
_____ that the audience
was convinced.
   a. ambiguous
   b. tenuous
   c. trenchant
   d. reactionary
   e. foolish

10. The water was from all the activity of the porpoises.
   a. lazy
   b. tranquil
   c. sinking
   d. turbulent
   e. soothing

11. His _____ manners of-
fended the hostess.
   a. unnoticed
   b. uncovered
   c. undone
   d. immaterial
   e. uncouth

12. A conscientious employer does not
_____ a troublesome
employee in front of others.
   a. upbraid
   b. ignore
   c. praise
   d. upgrade
   e. cheer

13. A security guard needs to be extra
_____ on moonless
nights.
   a. chilly
   b. vigilant
   c. vibrant
   d. unfriendly
   e. hesitant

14. Because the sun regularly rises at
the same time of day from year to
year, its apparent action can be
said to be _____.
   a. recurrent
   b. recursive
   c. rectilinear
   d. rampant
   e. reactionary

15. Step-parents may exercise too little control over children for fear
that they are _____ the
rights of the child's natural parent.
   a. vanquishing
   b. vilifying
   c. usurping
   d. upbraiding
   e. truncating

Part V

MASTERY CHALLENGES 99–117

You have now had experience with many facets of the English language: building blocks and word elements; evolved and invented words; borrowed and foreign words; medical and legal terminology; verb forms, plurals, pronunciation, and spelling. Having built a power vocabulary, you should now be comfortable with using it in your speech and writing.

Part V is devoted to Mastery Challenges, reinforcing your command of the language and testing your power vocabulary.

Mastery Challenges 67–75

For each challenge, circle the word or phrase that means most nearly the same as the key word.

Challenge 67

1. abbreviate
   a. shorten
   b. cure
   c. complete
   d. mitigate

2. abeyance
   a. distance
   b. leave-taking
   c. postponement
   d. hatred

3. abjure
   a. swear
   b. legislate
   c. remember
   d. renounce

4. abnegate
   a. forget
   b. deny
   c. prevent
   d. damage

5. abortive
   a. stuttering
   b. illegal
   c. deadening
   d. ineffectual

6. abridge
   a. cross over
   b. shorten
   c. extend
   d. circumvent

197

7. abscond
    a. forgive
    b. abstain
    c. cut and slash
    d. steal and flee

8. abstemious
    a. picky
    b. moderate
    c. unpleasant
    d. demanding

9. accede
    a. proceed
    b. precede
    c. prevent
    d. consent

10. accept
    a. exclude
    b. admit
    c. scrutinize
    d. anticipate

11. acclaim
    a. deny
    b. procure
    c. applaud
    d. denounce

12. accumulate
    a. gather
    b. compute
    c. expurgate
    d. release from prison

13. acquit
    a. walk out
    b. condemn
    c. set free
    d. apply for

14. adduce
    a. provide reasons
    b. compute
    c. suspect
    d. imply

15. adulation
    a. condemnation
    b. derision
    c. praise
    d. fretfulness

16. advent
    a. arrival
    b. springtime
    c. rental
    d. perusal

17. advocate
    a. speak to
    b. warn
    c. plead for
    d. scold

18. affirmation
    a. avowal
    b. confirmation
    c. denial
    d. strengthening

19. affluent
    a. gaseous
    b. well-spoken
    c. wealthy
    d. esoteric

20. aggregate
    a. sum
    b. irritate
    c. breach
    d. division

Challenge 68

1. averse
   a. eloquent
   b. lying across
   c. reluctant
   d. gregarious

2. baneful
   a. unhappy
   b. morose
   c. evil
   d. obstreperous

3. beguile
   a. deceive
   b. wander
   c. fling
   d. harass

4. belie
   a. rest
   b. excuse
   c. prove false
   d. make appropriate

5. berate
   a. scold
   b. score
   c. confuse
   d. confute

6. biped
   a. two-wheeled
   b. side-swiped
   c. two-footed
   d. half-witted

7. blithe
   a. cheerful
   b. thin
   c. addle-brained
   d. stubborn

8. breach
   a. extenuate
   b. attenuate
   c. gap
   d. bridge

9. burgeon
   a. sprout
   b. bunion
   c. burnish
   d. bury

10. cadence
    a. dialect
    b. discordance
    c. rhythmic flow
    d. harmonics

11. calumniate
    a. plaster
    b. slander
    c. complement
    d. compliment

12. candor
    a. rudeness
    b. rancor
    c. frankness
    d. stealth

13. capacious
    a. skillful
    b. concealing
    c. greedy
    d. spacious

14. capitol
    a. wealth
    b. investment
    c. headquarters
    d. building

15. capitulate
    a. surrender
    b. decapitate
    c. invest
    d. demand

16. carnal
    a. of the body
    b. of the heart
    c. of the spirit
    d. of the mind

17. castigate
    a. chatter
    b. encourage
    c. criticize
    d. shut tight

18. cede
    a. lease
    b. acknowledge
    c. follow
    d. yield

19. celerity
    a. swiftness
    b. infamy
    c. wittiness
    d. acidity

20. censure
    a. retirement
    b. hundredth
    c. affirmation
    d. blame

Challenge 69

1. contentious
    a. honest
    b. adjoining
    c. catchy
    d. quarrelsome

2. contingent
    a. contiguous
    b. cerebral
    c. celebration
    d. depending upon

3. contravene
    a. intercept
    b. interrupt
    c. approve
    d. oppose

4. convene
    a. help
    b. assemble
    c. monitor
    d. interpolate

5. convoke
    a. rebuke
    b. recall
    c. compose
    d. summon

6. corpulent
    a. deceased
    b. obese
    c. flesh-eating
    d. circular

7. corrigible
    a. corroded
    b. eroded
    c. malleable
    d. reformable

8. countermand
    a. invoke
    b. revoke an order
    c. slap
    d. retired

9. credence
   a. harmony
   b. religion
   c. orthodoxy
   d. belief

10. credulous
    a. trustworthy
    b. gullible
    c. believable
    d. fatuous

11. dearth
    a. mortality
    b. scarcity
    c. morbidity
    d. secrecy

12. debauch
    a. dehydrate
    b. steal away
    c. remove
    d. corrupt

13. deceive
    a. send back
    b. trick
    c. forget
    d. admonish

14. deduce
    a. lead away
    b. reason
    c. topple
    d. confuse

15. deference
    a. indifference
    b. mockery
    c. removal
    d. respect

16. degenerate
    a. destitute
    b. decline
    c. debilitate
    d. devolve

17. delete
    a. please
    b. pontificate
    c. alter
    d. erase

18. demagogue
    a. teacher
    b. manipulative leader
    c. wily politician
    d. populist

19. demote
    a. harmonize
    b. mobilize
    c. lower in rank
    d. raise in value

20. denigrate
    a. defame
    b. assign
    c. deny
    d. renounce

Challenge 70

1. facile
   a. quick
   b. inexpensive
   c. deceptive
   d. expert

2. fatuous
   a. obnoxiously foolish
   b. excessively generous
   c. obese
   d. gaseous

3. flammable
   a. fire-proof
   b. kiln-dried
   c. capable of being ignited
   d. igneous

4. fluctuate
   a. erupt
   b. guess
   c. worry
   d. vary

5. generic
   a. communicable
   b. esoteric
   c. pertaining to race or kind
   d. variegated

6. gratuitous
   a. thankful
   b. inexpensive
   c. dubious
   d. free

7. heinous
   a. ridiculous
   b. atrocious
   c. of the blood
   d. somber

8. herald
   a. announce departure
   b. special delivery
   c. forecast
   d. announce

9. heterodox
   a. paradoxical
   b. nonconforming
   c. dilemma
   d. imperturbable

10. hindsight
    a. prescience
    b. overseeing
    c. foreboding
    d. looking backwards

11. homogeneous
    a. similarly shaped
    b. variegated
    c. male gender
    d. uniform throughout

12. hyperbole
    a. boomerang
    b. overlooked
    c. overwhelmed
    d. exaggeration

13. ignominious
    a. flammable
    b. disgraceful
    c. unschooled
    d. highly explosive

14. illicit
    a. draw out
    b. barely perceivable
    c. not necessary
    d. not licensed

15. impeccable
    a. persnickety
    b. faultless
    c. painstaking
    d. unadulterated

16. impediment
    a. cavity
    b. aperture
    c. luggage
    d. obstacle

17. imperative
    a. subjective
    b. of great importance
    c. belonging to emperors
    d. minuscule

18. impervious
    a. accepting
    b. hopeful
    c. unwilling
    d. impenetrable

19. importune
    a. curse
    b. beg
    c. impose
    d. suppose

20. inadvertence
    a. inaccuracy
    b. happenstance
    c. willful
    d. oversight

Challenge 71

1. kindred
    a. related
    b. one thousandth
    c. teased
    d. approximate

2. lacerate
    a. cover with oil
    b. chew
    c. tear roughly
    d. fling

3. legacy
    a. summons
    b. inheritance
    c. written document
    d. affidavit

4. liable
    a. deceptive
    b. owned by
    c. prone
    d. exposed to

5. litigation
    a. fury
    b. lawsuit
    c. constraint
    d. happenstance

6. lucid
    a. ridiculous
    b. lightweight
    c. transparent
    d. not bound

7. lugubrious
    a. mournful
    b. laughable
    c. deeply cut
    d. accented

8. magnate
    a. attractive
    b. great-hearted
    c. beggar
    d. important business person

9. malfeasance
    a. wrongdoing
    b. maliciousness
    c. disowning
    d. sorrowfulness

10. manifest
    a. make clear
    b. holiday
    c. varied
    d. make straight

11. matrix
    a. queen
    b. survivor
    c. mold
    d. highway

12. median
    a. middle
    b. maximum
    c. foreign
    d. poorly constructed

13. meretricious
    a. praiseworthy
    b. dishonest
    c. superficially attractive
    d. impecunious

14. militate
    a. work against
    b. arm
    c. attack
    d. debate

15. miscellany
    a. annotations
    b. itinerary
    c. collection of unlike things
    d. foolishness

16. mnemonics
    a. memory development
    b. forgetfulness
    c. ammunition
    d. pain-killers

17. morass
    a. field
    b. mountain range
    c. inundation
    d. swamp

18. mores
    a. plenitude
    b. customs
    c. surplus
    d. morale

19. mutation
    a. silence
    b. purification
    c. flux
    d. change

20. negate
    a. mock
    b. make ineffective
    c. transmute
    d. weigh down

Challenge 72

1. neophyte
   a. retiree
   b. specialist
   c. new convert
   d. heterodox

2. nihilism
   a. disbelief
   b. death
   c. socialism
   d. conversion

3. nomenclature
   a. inaccurate names
   b. ruling
   c. technical names
   d. marriage

4. non sequitur
   a. illogical conclusion
   b. no exit
   c. nonconformist
   d. illegal transaction

5. noxious
   a. repulsive
   b. unkind
   c. injurious
   d. evil

6. obliterate
   a. demolish
   b. cloud
   c. forget
   d. cover up

7. obscure
   a. powerful
   b. threatening
   c. murky
   d. preoccupied

8. obstreperous
   a. boisterous
   b. infected
   c. stubborn
   d. uninvited

9. obtuse
   a. foreshortened
   b. frozen
   c. dull
   d. whirling

10. onus
    a. responsibility
    b. aperture
    c. exclamation
    d. monotone

11. orbicular
    a. of the age
    b. of the feet
    c. circular
    d. rectangular

12. ostentatious
    a. pretentious
    b. deep voiced
    c. animated
    d. retiring

13. panacea
    a. illogical statement
    b. tranquility
    c. cure-all
    d. belief in God

14. pantoscopic
    a. panoramic
    b. chaotic
    c. omniscient
    d. underwater

15. paraphrase
    a. quote
    b. joke
    c. rewording
    d. attribution

16. partisan
    a. devoted to a cause
    b. many-colored
    c. dubious
    d. fragmented

17. pedantic
    a. hiker
    b. extravagantly wealthy
    c. intellectual showing-off
    d. jaywalker

18. penurious
    a. stingy
    b. slow-moving
    c. ancient
    d. happy-go-lucky

19. peremptory
    a. judicial
    b. decreed
    c. imperative
    d. unnecessary

20. permeable
    a. penetrable by fluids
    b. transferrable
    c. translucent
    d. impervious

Challenge 73

1. ratio
   a. proportion
   b. height
   c. duplicity
   d. division

7. relegate
   a. enact as law
   b. reread
   c. assign to lower position
   d. turn over

2. rebuttal
   a. knock again
   b. refusal
   c. contradiction
   d. controversy

8. reprehend
   a. blame
   b. remember
   c. grasp
   d. eject

3. recapitulate
   a. invade
   b. procure
   c. summarize
   d. truncate

9. reprove
   a. invent
   b. bolster
   c. censure
   d. debate

4. reconcile
   a. bring to agreement
   b. reconsider
   c. ponder
   d. bring to fruition

10. rescind
    a. cancel
    b. burn
    c. raise
    d. return

5. recriminate
   a. incarcerate
   b. reprobate
   c. counter-accuse
   d. countermand

11. retain
    a. give back
    b. wear constantly
    c. keep
    d. cleanse

6. refrain
   a. avoid doing
   b. sing
   c. paraphrase
   d. accept only

12. retrogress
    a. lose ground
    b. return
    c. diminish
    d. spiral

13. sanctimony
    a. holiness
    b. orthodoxy
    c. false piety
    d. vocation

14. secular
    a. not religious
    b. naval
    c. sanctimonious
    d. unorthodox

15. simultaneous
    a. chronological
    b. temporal
    c. at the same time
    d. permanent

16. sonorous
    a. resonant
    b. snoring
    c. whispered
    d. silent

17. stoical
    a. frivolous
    b. morbid
    c. calmly strong
    d. worried

18. strident
    a. harsh-sounding
    b. brisk
    c. long-legged
    d. gregarious

19. subcutaneous
    a. beneath the rose
    b. underground
    c. beneath the skin
    d. submerged

20. suffuse
    a. overspread
    b. inject
    c. suppress
    d. welter

Challenge 74

1. supercilious
    a. absentminded
    b. haughty
    c. punctual
    d. jovial

2. supersede
    a. run ahead
    b. contradict
    c. fly above
    d. take the place of

3. surreptitious
    a. sleeping
    b. clandestine
    c. flawed
    d. careful

4. tacitly
    a. politely
    b. with few words
    c. stealthily
    d. by implication

5. temporize
    a. count
    b. delay
    c. order
    d. select

6. terse
    a. loquacious
    b. mumbled
    c. to the point
    d. harmonious

7. traduce
   a. put into a trance
   b. cheat
   c. introduce
   d. slander

8. transitory
   a. affixed
   b. fleeting
   c. dreamy
   d. crosswise

9. transverse
   a. carried
   b. broken into parts
   c. obtuse
   d. lying across

10. tribulation
    a. acclaim
    b. great trouble
    c. great reward
    d. branching out

11. turgid
    a. slow
    b. stubborn
    c. furious
    d. swollen

12. umbrage
    a. cloudiness
    b. touchiness
    c. spreading out
    d. rank growth

13. unilateral
    a. one-level
    b. wholesome
    c. undivided
    d. one-sided

14. unprecedented
    a. not planned
    b. never done before
    c. without warning
    d. totally forgotten

15. vacillation
    a. prevention
    b. whiskers
    c. fluttering in the wind
    d. fluctuation of mind

16. variable
    a. multiplied
    b. many-parted
    c. changing
    d. stable

17. verbose
    a. wordy
    b. hand-written
    c. terse
    d. eloquent

18. vertex
    a. dizziness
    b. nadir
    c. apex
    d. median

19. viability
    a. capacity to live
    b. able to laugh
    c. true-to-life
    d. capacity

20. vicissitude
    a. likeness
    b. misery
    c. ups and downs
    d. foresightedness

Challenge 75

1. superfluous
   a. rapidly flowing
   b. very bright
   c. extra
   d. necessary

2. supplicate
   a. beg
   b. replace
   c. provide
   d. bend gently

3. synthesis
   a. phony
   b. collection
   c. combination of parts into whole
   d. splitting

4. tedious
   a. boring
   b. minute
   c. child-like
   d. melodious

5. tenable
   a. capable of being defended
   b. swift
   c. inhabitable
   d. capable of withstanding pain

6. tractable
   a. arable
   b. fertile
   c. easily led
   d. easily broken

7. transgression
   a. breaking the law
   b. greeting
   c. extending
   d. willfulness

8. transmute
   a. change direction
   b. change color
   c. change form
   d. change money

9. trepidation
   a. trembling
   b. fortitude
   c. stumbling
   d. hazard

10. truncate
    a. plant
    b. cut in pieces
    c. cut short
    d. put into containers

11. ubiquity
    a. omnipresence
    b. impudence
    c. sinfulness
    d. curiosity

12. undulating
    a. softening
    b. splitting
    c. waving
    d. burying

13. unmitigated
    a. not lessened
    b. not sent
    c. without stop
    d. not understood

14. urbane
    a. from the city
    b. sneaky
    c. smoothly polite
    d. rough-edged

15. vacuous
    a. empty
    b. hungry
    c. naive
    d. opened

16. verbatim
    a. forbidden
    b. paraphrased
    c. translated
    d. word for word

17. verisimilitude
    a. twinhood
    b. appearance of truth
    c. approaching perfection
    d. cheerfulness

18. vestige
    a. clothing
    b. property
    c. wordiness
    d. remnant

19. vicarious
    a. hilarious
    b. experienced secondhand
    c. remembered
    d. spiteful

20. vilify
    a. spy out
    b. spear through
    c. revitalize
    d. defame

Part VI

A GLOSSARY OF WORD ELEMENTS

A

a- *without, not* (see *in-, un-, non-*; variant form *an-*) amoral, atonal, atheist

ab- *away, from* (see *apo-*) abstract, abject, abrasive, abnormal

-able *like, capable of being* (see *-ible, -ile*) lovable, movable, portable, tenable

-ac *like, pertaining to* (see *-ous, -ine, -ic, -ical, -ive*) insomniac, cardiac

acr- *sharp* (see *acu-*) acrimonious, exacerbate, acerbic

acro- *high* (see *alti-*) acrobat, acropolis, acronym

acou- *hearing, sound* (see *son-, phon-, aud-*) acoustical, acouesthesia

act- *to make, do* (see *ag-, fac-, fic-*) action, active, reactionary, counteract

acu- *sharp* (see *acr-*) acumen, acute, acupuncture

-acy *act or quality of* (see *-ism, -ation, -tion, -ure, -ment, -tude*) tenancy, infancy, literacy, accuracy

ad- *to, toward* adhere, adjunct, admit, advertise

adelph- *brother* (see *frater-*) Philadelphia

ag- *to make, do* (see *act-, fac-, fic-,*; variant form *ig-*) agitate, agency, cogitate

-age *state or quality of* (see *-ry, -hood, -ship, -ness, -ity, -cy, -ance, -ence, -ia*) dotage, bondage, courage

agon- *struggle* agonize, agony, protagonist

211

ali-   *other, another* (see *hetero-, alter-*) alibi, alienate

alter-   *other, another* (see *hetero-, ali-*) alternate, altruist, altercation

alti-   *high* (see *acro-*) altitude, altar, alto

ami-   *friend* amicable, amigo

ambu-   *to walk* (see *patet-*) ambulatory, ambulance, amble

ambi-   *both* (variant form *amphi-*) ambidextrous, ambivalent, ambiversion

amor-   *love* (see *phil-*) enamored

amphi-   *both* (variant form *ambi-*) amphitheater, amphora

-an   *belonging to* (see *-ary, -ory*) urban, agrarian, American

an-   *without, not* (see *a-, in-, un-, non-*) anaerobic, analgesic, anarchy

-ance   *state or quality of* (see *-ry, -hood, -ship, -ness, -age, -ity, -cy, -ence, -ia*) dominance, resistance, radiance

anima-   *spirit* (see *noia-, psych-*) animal, equanimity, animation

ann-   *year* (variant form *enn-*) centennial, biennial, anniversary

-ant   *one who* (see *-er, -ar, -ary, -or, -ent, -ist*) tenant, supplicant, defendant, participant

ante-   *before, toward* (see *fore-, pre-, pro-*) antedate, antedeluvian, antecedent

anthro-   *man* (see *vir-, homo-;* variant form *andr-*) misanthropic, philanthropist, polyandry

anti-   *against* (see *contra-, counter-, ob-, with-*) antidote, antigen, antiphony, antithesis, antisocial

apo-   *away, from* (see *ab-*) apoplexy, apogee, apostle

aqua-   *water* (see *hydro-*) aquamarine, aqueduct, aquarium

-ar   *one who* (see *-er, -ary, -or, -ent, -ant, -ist*) scholar, peddlar, beggar

arch- (1) *ruler, leader* (see *-gogue*) monarch, anarchy, archangel

arch- (2) *first, most* (see *primo-, proto-*) archbishop, archenemy, archeology

-ary (1) *one who* (see *-er, -ar, -or, -ent, -ant, -ist*) visionary, missionary, emissary, revolutionary

-ary (2) *belonging to* (see *-ory, -an*) secondary, contrary, temporary, sedentary, sanitary

astr- *star* (see *stell-*; variant form *aster-*) astrologist, astronomy, asterisk, disaster

-ate *to make* (see *-en, -ize, -fy*) enervate, participate, fabricate, captivate, saturate

-ation *act or quality of* (see *-ism, -ure, -tion, -ment, -acy, -itude*) demonstration, divination, tabulation

aud- *hearing, sound* (see *son-, phon-, acou-*) audience, auditory, auditor, auditorium

auto- *self* (see *sui-*) automobile, autobiography, automotive

aug- *to increase* (see *cre-*; variant form *aux-*) author, auction, auxiliary

B

belli- *war* belligerent, rebellion, rebel

bene- *good, well* (see *well-, bon-, eu-*) benevolent, beneficial, benediction

bi- *two* (variant forms *du-, di-*) binary, bicycle, biped, bigamy

biblio- *book* (see *lib-*) bibliophile, Bible, bibliomania

bio- *life* (see *zoo-, viv-, vit-*) biology, biosphere, bionic

bon- *good, well* (see *well-, bene-, eu-*) bonny, boon, bonanza

brev- *short* abbreviate, brief, breviary

C

cad- *to fall* (see *cid-, cas-*) decadent, cadaver, cadent

cap- (1) *head* capital, capitulate, decapitate

cap-   (2) *to take, hold* (see *cep-*) captivate, capable, captor

card-   *heart* (see *cord-*) myocardial, pericardium, cardiovascular

carn-   *body, flesh* (see *corp-, soma-*) carnage, carnival, carnal, incarnate

cas-   *to fall* (see *cad-, cid-*) casualty, cast, casual

cata-   *down, from* (see *de-*) cataract, catacombs, cataclysm

caust-   *to burn* (variant form *caut-*) holocaust, cauterize, encaustic

ced-   *to go* (see *ces-*) secede, recede, intercede

celer-   *fast* celerity, decelerate

cent-   *hundred* (see *hect-*) centennial, cents, centigrade

cep-   *to take, hold* (see *cap-*) intercept, concept, reception

ces-   *to go* (see *ced-*) secession, recess, recessional

cess-   *to separate* cessation, abscess, access, decease, concession

chiro-   *hand* (see *manu-*) chiropractor, chiromancy, chiropodist

chron-   *time* (see *tempor-*) synchronize, anachronism, chronic, chronicle

comp-   *to fill* complement, compliment, comply

con-   *with, together* (see *syn-, com-*) concert, confection, conflagration, contemporary

contra-   *against* (see *anti-, counter-, ob-, with-*) contraband, contradict, contrary

cord-   *heart* (see *card-*) record, accord, discord, concord

corp-   *body, flesh* (see *carn-, soma-*) corpse, corpuscle, incorporate

cosm-   *world, universe* cosmos, cosmetics, cosmopolitan

counter-   *against* (see *anti-, contra-, ob-, with-*) countermand, counterculture, counterintelligence

-cracy   *government by, rule* theocracy, meritocracy, plutocracy

cre-   *to grow* (see *aug-*) crescent, crescendo, increase, procreate

cred-   *to believe* incredulous, credit, credential

cryo-   *cold* cryogen, cryotherapy, cryostat

crypt-   *hidden* crypt, cryptogram, cryptography

culp-   *to blame* culpable, exculpate, culpability

cumb-   *to lie down* (variant form *cub-*) incumbent, succumb, incubator

cur-   *to care* cure, curator, pedicure, sinecure

curr-   *to run* (see *curs-*) recurrent, current, currency, curriculum

curs-   *to run* (see *curr-*) precursor, cursive, cursorial, cursory

cut-   *skin* (see *derm-*) subcutaneous, cutaneous

cycl-   *circle* (see *orb-*) cyclone, Cyclops, cyclical

D

dat-   *to give* (see *don-*, *dot-*) data, date, dative

de-   *down, from* (see *cata-*) depose, deject, decrease

deb-   *to owe* debt, debenture, debit

dec-   *ten* decimate, decade, December, decimal

dei-   *God* (see *theo-*; variant form *div-*) deity, deism, divine

demi-   *half* (see *hemi-*, *semi-*) demitasse, demiurge

demo-   *people* (see *pleb-*, *pop-*) epidemic, endemic, democracy

derm-   *skin* (see *cut-*) dermatologist, hypodermic, ectoderm

di-   *two* (variant forms *du-*, *bi-*) digress, diphthong, dioxide

dia-   (1) *day* (see *jour-*; variant form *diu-*) dial, dismal

dia-   (2) *through, across* (see *trans-, per-*) diagonal, dialogue, diagram

dic-   *to speak, talk, say* (see *loqu-, loc-, voc-, cit-*) diction, predict, edict, malediction

dis-   *wrong, bad* (see *mal-, mis-*; variant forms *dif-, dys-*) disease, disable, disaster, difficult

doc-   *to teach* (see *tut-, tui-*) doctrine, docent, docile

dom-   *rule* dominion, domain, dominant

don-   *to give* (see *dat-, dot-*) donate, condone, pardon

dorm-   *sleep* (see *somn-, sopor-, hypno-, morph-, com-*) dormant, dormer

dot-   *to give* (see *don-, dat-*; variant form *dos-*) dose, anecdote

dox-   *opinion* heterodox, doxology, paradox

du-   *two* (variant forms *di-, bi-*) dual, duplex, duplicate

duc-   *to lead* conduct, ductile, educe, produce, duchess

dur-   *hard* obdurate, endure, duress

dynam-   *power* hydrodynamics, dynamite, dynasty

E

e-   *out of, outside* (see *ecto-, ex-, extra-*) elect, eject, evoke

ecto-   *out of, outside* (see *e-, ex-, extra-*) ectopic, ectoplasm, ectomorphic

ego-   *I* egoist, egotistical, egomania

en-   *in, into, within* (see *in, intr-, endo-,*; variant form *em-*) embrace, parenthesis, encage

-en   *to make* (see *-ate, -ize, -fy*) quicken, stiffen, weaken, harden

-ence   *state or quality of* (see *-ry, -hood, -ship, -ness, -age, -ity, -cy, -ance, -ia*) dependence, competence, residence

endo-   *in, into, within* (see *in-, intr-, en-*) endocrine, endogamy, endogenous

-ent   *one who* (see *-er, -ar, -ary, -or, -ant, -ist*) president, regent, resident

epi-   *on* epicycle, epilogue, epigram, epitaph

equi-   *equal* (see *par-*) equitable, equity, equivocate

-er   *one who* (see *-ar, -ary, -or, -ent, -ant- -ist*) worker, lawyer, carpenter

err-   *to wander* (see *migr-*) erroneous, error, aberration

(a)esthe-   *to feel* esthetics, anaesthesia, esthete, synesthesia

eu-   *good, well* (see *well-, bene-, bon-*) euphemism, euphonious, euphoria, eulogy

ev-   *time, age* (see *chron-, tempor-*) primeval, longevity

ex-   *out of, outside* (see *e-, ecto-, extra-*; variant from *ec-*) exit, exotic, ecstasy

extra-   (1) *out of, outside* (see *e-, ex-, ecto-*) external, extrinsic, exterior, extraneous

extra-   (2) *beyond* (see *para-, meta-, ultra-*) extraterrestrial, extrapolate, extravagant

F

fac-   *to make, do* (see *ag-, act-, fic-*) factory, factual, facade

fal-   *to deceive* false, fallacy, infallible

fer-   *to bring, carry* (see *port-*) ferry, refer, fertile, conference

fic-   *to make, do* (see *ag-, act-, fac-*) beneficial, fictile, fictitious

-fic   *causing* terrific, beatific, specific

fid-   *faith* (see *tru-*; variant forms *fed-, feal-*) confide, infidel, fiduciary, perfidy, federal, fealty

fil-   *son* affiliate, filiation

fin-   *end* (see *term-*) define, finish, final

flam- *fire* (see *pyro-*, *ign-*) flame, flamboyant, inflammatory

flec- *to bend* (variant form *flex-*) flexible, reflection, inflection

flu- *to flow* (see *fluv-*) fluid, superfluous

fluv- *to flow* (see *flu-*) flux, fluvial, influenza

fore- *before, toward* (see *pre-*, *ante-*, *pro-*) foreword, foretell, forebear

form- *to shape* formative, reform, conformity

fort- *strong* (see *vali-*; variant form *forc-*) fortitude, comfort, fortress, forcible

fract- *to break* (see *rupt-*, *frag-*) fraction, refract, fractious

frag- *to break* (see *rupt-*, *frac-*) fragile, fragmentary, frail

frater- *brother* (see *adelph-*) confraternity, fraternal, fraternize

fug- *to flee* refuge, fugue, centrifugal

fus- *to pour* suffuse, fuse

-fy *to make* (see *-en*, *-ate*, *-ize*) magnify, dignify, horrify

G

gen- *origin, birth* genetics, primogeniture, generate, homogenized

geo- *earth* (see *terr-*) geologist, geography, geocentric

ger- *old* (see *paleo-*, *vet-*, *sen-*) gerontology, gerontocracy

-gogue *ruler, leader* (see *arch-*) pedagogue, synagogue, hypnagogic

glyph- *carving* (see *sculp-*) petroglyph, anaglyph, glyptic

gnos- *to know, learn* (see *cogn-*, *sci-*, *sent-*, *sens-*, *wit-*) gnome, prognosis, diagnosis

grad- *to move forward* (see *gress-*) gradual, gradation, grade

gram- *writing* (see *scrip-*, *graph-*, *scrib-*) epigram, diagram, grammar

graph- *writing* (see *scrip-*, *gram-*, *scrib-*) graphite, telegraph, phonograph

grat- *pleasing* gratitude, grateful, congratulate, gratuity

grav- *heavy* gravity, grave, gravitate

greg- *crowd* gregarious, egregious, segregate

gress- *to move forward* (see *grad-*) regression, egress, digress

gyn- *woman* gynecology, polygyny, gynocracy

gyr- *to whirl, spin* (see *turb-*) gyroscope, gyre, gyrocompass

H

hect- *hundred* (see *cent-*) hecatomb, hecameter, hecagraph

helio- *sun* (see *sol-*) perihelion, helium, heliotrope

hemi- *half* (see *demi-*, *semi-*) hemicycle, hemihedral

hepta- *seven* (see *sept-*) heptameter, heptavalent

her- *to cling* (see *hes-*) coherence, inherent

hes- *to cling* (see *her-*) hesitate, adhesive, cohesive

hetero- *other, another* (see *ali-*, *alter-*) heterosexual, heterogeneous, heterodyne

hexa- *six* (see *sex-*) hexahedron, hexagram, hexapod

hibit- *to hold in* (variant form *habit-*) exhibit, prohibit, inhabit

hier- *holy, sacred* (see *sacr-*, *sanct-*) hierarchy, hierophant, hierocracy

holo- *whole* hologram, holography, catholic

homo- (1) *same* (see *simul-*) homogenize, homonym, homosexual

homo- (2) *man* (see *anthr-*, *vir-*) homo sapiens

-hood *state or quality of* (see *-ry*, *-ship*, *-ness*, *-age*, *-ity*, *-cy*, *-ance*, *-ence*, *-ia*) brotherhood, neighborhood, manhood

hydro- *water* (see *aqua-*) hydrodynamics, hydrophobia, hydraulic, hydrant

hyper-   *above, over* (see *super-*) hyperactive, hyperbole, hypertension

hypno-   *sleep* (see *dorm-, somn-, sopor-, morph-, com-*) hypnogogic, hypnosis

hypo-   *under, below* (see *sub-, infra-*) hypotenuse, hypocrisy

I

-ia   *state or quality of* (see *-ry, -hood, -ship, -ness, -age, -ity, -cy, -ance, -ence*) anemia, pneumonia, mania

-ian   *rank or status* magician, optician

iatr-   *healing* iatrogenic, podiatry, geriatric

-ible   *like, capable of being* (see *-able, -ile*) permissible, audible, visible, intangible

-ic   *like, pertaining to* (see *-ous, -ine, -ical, -ive, -ac*) dramatic, heroic, rustic, optic

-ical   *like, pertaining to* (see *-ous, -ine, -ic, -ive, -ac*) comical, theatrical, spherical

ign-   *fire* (see *flam-, pyro-*) ignition, igneous

ile   *like, capable of being* (see *-able, -ible;* variant form *-il*) puerile, juvenile, facile

in-   (1) *in, into, within* (see *intr-, endo-, en-*) inject, inhibit, infuse

in-   (2) *without, not* (see *a-, an-, non-, un-*) incapable, insensitive, incoherent, infidel, incredible

-ine   *like, pertaining to* (see *-ous, -ic, -ical, -ive, -ac*) masculine, feminine, saline

infra-   *under, below* (see *sub-, hypo-*) infrared, infrasonic, inferior

inter-   *between* (variant form *enter-*) intercept, intermission, enterprise

intr-   *in, into, within* (see *in-, endo-, en-*) intramural, intracostal, introduce

-ish   *resembling* (see *-some, -like, -ly, -oid*) foolish, selfish, sheepish

-ism   *act or quality of* (see *-ation, -urge, -tion, -ment, -acy, -itude*) terrorism, materialism, dogmatism, pantheism

-ist   *one who* (see *-er, -ar, -ary, -or, -ent, -ant*) artist, misogynist, radiologist

-itude   *act or quality of* (see *-ism, -ation, -ure, -tion, -ment, -acy*) fortitude, amplitude, beatitude

-ity   *state or quality of* (see *-ry, -hood, -ship, -ness, -age, -cy, -ance, -ence, -ia*) nobility, clarity, hilarity

-ive   *like, pertaining to* (see *-ous, -ine, -ic, -ical, -ac*) explosive, productive, counteractive

-ize   *to make* (see *-en, -ate, -fy*) maximize, realize, fertilize, revitalize

J

jac-   *to throw* (see *jec-*) adjacent, jactation

jec-   *to throw* (see *jac-*) trajectory, eject, projection

joc-   *to jest* joke, jocose, juggler

jour-   *day* (see *dia-*) journal, adjourn, journalism

junct-   *to join* adjunct, junction, juncture, conjunction

jur-   *to swear* jury, abjure, jurisprudence

K

kilo-   *thousand* (see *mill-*) kilowatt, kiloton, kilometer

kine-   *to move* (see *mot-, mov-, mob-;* variant form *cine-*) cinema, kinesiology, kinesthesia

L

labor-   *to work* (see *oper-*) laborious, labor, laboratory

laud-   *to praise* applaud, plausible, plaudit

lat-   *wide* dilate

lect-   *to read, choose* (see *leg-*) elect, lecture, select

leg-   *to read, choose* (see *lect-;* variant form *lig-*) legend, diligent, intelligent

len-   *soft* (see *moll-*) relentless, lenient

lib-   (1) *book* (see *biblio-*) libretto, libel

lib-   (2) *free* (variant form *liv-*) liberty, deliver, liberal

-like   *resembling* (see *-some, -ly, -ish, -oid*) lifelike, ladylike

lith-   *stone* (see *petr-*) lithosphere, monolith, paleolithic

loc-   (1) *to speak, talk, say* (see *dic-, loqu-, voc-, cit-*) interlocutor, circumlocution, locution

loc-   (2) *place* (see *top-, stead-*) local, locate, locomotive

logy-   *study, word* (variant form *logue-*) astrology, logic, monologue

loqu-   *to speak, talk, say* (see *dic-, loc-, voc-, cit-*) eloquent, ventriloquist, soliloquy

luc-   *light* (see *lum-, photo-*) translucent, Lucia, Lucifer, lucent

lucr-   *money* (see *pecun-*) lucre

lud-   *game* (variant form *lus-*) interlude, delude, collusion

lum-   *light* (see *luc-, photo-*) luminous, lumen, luminescence

lun-   *moon* (see *mon-*) lunatic, lunate, lunette

-ly   *resembling* (see *-ish, -like, -some, -oid*) slowly, happily, sleepily

M

macro-   *large, great* (see *magn-, maxi-, mega-*) macrocosm, macroeconomics, macrobiotic, macron

magn-   *large, great* (see *macro-, maxi, mega-*) magnate, magnificent, magnify

mal-   *wrong, bad* (see *dis-, mis-*) malformed, malevolent, malefactor, dismal

manu- *hand* (see *chiro-*) manual, manacle, manuscript

mar- *sea* (variant form *mer-*) maritime, marine, mariner, mermaid

mater- *mother* matron, matrimony, matriarch, metropolis

maxi- *large, great* (see *magn-, macro-, mega-*) maximize, maxim, maximal

medi- *middle* (see *meso-*) Mediterranean, medieval, mediator

mega- *large, great* (see *magn-, macro-, maxi-*) megalomania, megaton, megacycle

mens- *to measure* (see *meter-*) immense, commensurate

-ment *act or quality of* (see *-ism, -ation, -ure, -tion, -acy, -itude*) contentment, excitement, abasement

meso- *middle* (see *medi-*) Mesopotamia, mesoderm

meta- *beyond* (see *extra-, para-, ultra-*) metaphysics, metabolism, metaphor

meter- *to measure* (see *mens-*; variant form *metr-*) metric, tachometer, symmetrical

micro- *small* (see *min-*) microbe, microphone, microfilm

migr- *to wander* (see *err-*) emigration, immigrant, migratory

mill- *thousand* (see *kilo-*) millisecond, millenium, million

min- *small* (see *micro-*) minimum, minority, diminish

mis- (1) *wrong, bad* (see *mal-, dis-*) misspelling, mistake, misrepresent

mis- (2) *to send* (see *mit-*) missive, admission, missionary

mit- *to send* (see *mis-*) permit, admit, remit

mne- *to remember* amnesty, mnemonics

mob- *to move* (see *mov-, mot-, kine-*) automobile, immobility, mob

moll- *soft* (see *len-*) mollify, mollusk

mon- (1) *moon* (see *lun-*; variant form *men-*) Monday, menstrual

mon- (2) *to warn, remind* premonition, monument, monitor

mono- *one* (see *uni-*, *sol-*) monologue, monocle, monarch, monolith, monogram

mori- *death* (see *mort-*, *thana-*) morbid

morph- (1) *form, shape* morphology, amorphous, morpheme

morph- (2) *sleep* (see *dorm-*, *sopor-*, *somn-*, *hypno-*, *com-*) Morpheus

mort- *death* (see *mori-*, *thana-*) mortuary, mortician, mortify, mortgage

mot- *to move* (see *mov-*, *mob-*, *kine-*) motor, motive, motivate, motion

mov- *to move* (see *mot-*, *mob-*, *kine-*) move, remove

multi- *many* (see *poly-*) multicolored, multiply, multitude

mur- *wall* intramural, immure

mut- *to change* mutable, permutation, commute

N

nat- *to be born* (variant form *nasc-*) natal, innate, nation, nascent, renaissance

nau- *ship* nausea, astronaut, nautilus

neg- *to deny* abnegation, negative, negotiate

neo- *new* (see *nov-*) neologism, neon, neophyte

-ness *state or quality of* (see *-ry*, *-hood*, *-ship*, *-age*, *-ity*, *-cy*, *-ance*, *-ence*, *-ia*) friendliness, kindness, quietness

nihil- *none, nothing* (see *null-*) nihilistic, nihility

noc- *to injure* (variant form *nox-*) noxious, innocuous, innocent, obnoxious

noct- *night* (variant form *nox-*) nocturne, noctilucent, equinox

noia *mind, spirit* (see *psych-*, *anima-*) metanoia

nom-   *name* (see *nym-*) nominal, nomenclature, nominee

nomy-   *to manage* economy, metronome, autonomy

non-   (1) *without, not* (see *un-, a-, an-, in-*) nontoxic, nonsense, none

non-   (2) *nine* (see *nov-*) nonagon, nonagenarian, noon

nov-   (1) *new* (see *neo-*) novel, novelty, innovation, renovate

nov-   (2) *nine* (see *non-*) November

null-   *none, nothing* (see *nihil-*) null, annul, nill

nym-   *name* (see *nom-*) synonym, antonym, homonym

O

ob-   *against* (see *anti-, contra-, counter-, with-*) obstruction, obdurate, object, obstacle

obliv-   *to forget* oblivion

octo-   *eight* October, octave, octagon

-oid   *resembling* (see *-some, -like, -ly, -ish*) humanoid, spheroid, asteroid

omni-   *all* (see *pan-*) omniscient, omnivorous, omnibus

oper-   *to work* (see *labor-*) opera, cooperate, operation

-or   *one who* (see *-ar, -ary, -er, -ent, -ant, -ist*) doctor, donor, investor

orb-   *circle* (see *cycl-*) exorbitant, orbicular, orb

ortho-   *straight* (see *rect-*) orthodoxy, orthography, orthopedics

-ory   *belonging to* (see *-ary, -an*) sensory, regulatory, promissory

-ose   *excessively* verbose, jocose, bellicose

-ous   *like, pertaining to* (see *-ine, -ic, -ical, -ive, -ac*) amorous, slanderous, tortuous

P

pac- *peace* peace, appease, pacifist

paleo- *old* (see *ger-*, *vet-*, *sen-*) paleolithic, paleography, paleontology

pan- *all* (see *omni-*) pandemonium, pantheon, pantomime

par- *equal* (see *equi-*) disparage, compare, par

para- *beyond* (see *extra-*, *meta-*, *ultra-*) paradox, parapsychology, parenthesis

pass- *feelings, suffering* (see *path-*) compassion, passionate, passive

pater- *father* repatriate, paternal, patronize

patet- *to walk* (see *ambu-*) path

path- *feelings, suffering* (see *pass-*) sympathetic, apathy, pathology

pecc- *sin* peccadillo, peccant, peccable

pecun- *money* (see *lucr-*) pecuniary, peculation

ped- (1) *foot* (see *pod-*, *pus-*) pedal, pedestal, pedestrian, impede

ped- (2) *child* pedagogue, pediatrician

pel- *to push, drive* (see *puls-*) compel, expel, impel

pend- *to hang, weigh* pendulum, pending, impending, pensive

penta- *five* (see *quint-*) pentangle, pentameter, pentathalon

per- *through, across* (see *dia-*, *trans-*) perceive, percent, perfect

peri- *around* (see *circum-*) pericardium, peripatetic, perihelion, perigee, periscope

peti- *to ask, seek* (see *quis-*, *quer-*, *rog-*) appetite, competitor, impetus

petr- *stone* (see *lith-*) petroleum, Peter, petrochemistry

phil- *love* (see *amor-*) philosophy, bibliophile, Philadelphia

phobia- *fear* phobic, claustrophobia, hydrophobia

phon- *hearing, sound* (see *son-, aud-, acou-*) phonetics, symphony, phonograph, cacophony

photo- *light* (see *lum-, luc-;* variant form *phos-*) photoluminescence, photon, phosphorous, phosphorescent

pleb- *people* (see *demo-, pop-*) plebiscite, plebe

plode- *to clap* implode, plosive

plor- *to cry out* (see *clam-*) explore, deplorable

plu- *more* plus, plurality, pluralistic

pod- *foot* (see *ped-, pus-*) podiatry, pseudopod, tripod

polis- *city* (see *polit-, civ-*) acropolis, megalopolis, police

polit- *city* (see *polis-, civ-*) politician, politics, cosmopolitan

poly- *many* (see *multi-*) polysyllabic, polyphonic, polytheism, polygon

pon- *to sit, stay, place* (see *posit-, sed-, sess-*) postpone, compound, depone

pop- *people* (see *demo-, pleb-*) populace, depopulate, popularity, populous

port- *to bring, carry* (see *fer-*) transport, deportation, report

posit- *to sit, stay, place* (see *pon-, sed-, sess-*) deposit, exposition, positive

post- *after* postdate, postpone, posthumous

poster- *behind* posterity, preposterous

pre- *before, toward* (see *fore-, ante-, pro-*) premonition, preview, preface, predict

primo- *first, most* (see *arch-, proto-*) primitive, primal, prime, primary

pro- *before, toward* (see *fore-, ante-, pre-*) program, project, prorate

proto- *first, most* (see *primo-, arch-*) proton, protozoa, protolithic

pseudo- *false* pseudopod, pseudoscience

psych- *mind, spirit* (see *noia-, anima-*) psychiatry, psychic, psychedelic

puls- *to push, drive* (see *pel-*) expulsion, compulsion, pulsing

purg- *to cleanse* purgative, purgatory, purge

pus- *foot* (see *ped-, pod-*) octopus, platypus

puta- *to consider* putative, impute, dispute

pyro- *fire* (see *flam-, ign-*) pyre, pyromaniac, pyretic

Q

quad- *four* (see *tetra-*; variant form *quart-*) quadruplets, quadrangle, quarter

quer- *to ask, seek* (see *peti-, quis-, rog-*; variant form *quir-*) query, inquire, require

quint- *five* (see *penta-*) quintet, quintessence

quis- *to ask, seek* (see *peti-, quer-, rog-*; variant form *ques-*) inquisitive, question, quiz, inquisition

R

radi- *ray* radiant, radial, radiation, radius

re- *back, again* reject, repeat, return, retreat, report

rect- *straight* (see *ortho-*) correct, rectify, direct

retro- *backwards* retroactive, retrogress, retrograde

rid- *to laugh* (see *ris-*) ridiculous, deride

ris- *to laugh* (see *rid-*) risible

rod- *to gnaw* (see *ros-*) erode

rog- *to ask, seek* (see *peti-, quis-, quer-*) arrogant, prerogative, derogatory

ros- *to gnaw* (see *rod-*) corrosion

rot- *to turn* (see *vert-*, *stroph-*) rotary, rotund, rotunda

rupt- *to break* (see *frag-*, *fract-*) erupt, interrupt, rupture, abrupt

-ry *state or quality of* (see *-hood, -ship, -ness, -age, -ity, -cy, -ance, -ence, -ia*) bigotry, revelry

S

sacr- *holy* (see *sanct-, hiero-*) sacrosanct, sacrilegious, sacred, sacrament

sag- *wise* (see *soph-*) sage, presage

sal- *to jump* (see *sault-, sult-;* variant form *sil-*) sally, assail, salacious, resilient

sanct- *holy* (see *sacr-, hiero-*) sanctuary, sanctify, sacrosanct

sat- *enough* saturate, satisfy, insatiable

sault- *to jump* (see *sult-, sal-*) somersault

scend- *to lean, climb* (see *clin-*) ascend, condescension

sci- *to think, know, sense* (see *sens-, sent-, cogn-, gnos-, wit-*) conscience, conscious

scop- *to see, look* (see *spec-, vid-, vis-, scrut-*) scope, microscopic

scrib- *writing* (see *scrip-, graph-, gram-*) prescribe, describe, ascribe

scrip- *writing* (see *graph-, gram-, scrib-*) inscription, scripture, script, manuscript

scrut- *to see, look* (see *spec-, vid, vis-, scop-*) scrutiny, scrutable, shrewd, scroll

sculp- *carving* (see *glyph-*) scalpel, sculpture

se- *aside, apart* secede, seclude, segregate, separate

sec- *to follow* (see *sequ-*) persecute, prosecute, execute

sect- *to cut* (variant form *sec-*) dissect, secant, intersection, section

sed- *to sit, stay, place* (see *pon-, posit-, sess-*) sediment, preside, residence

sess-   *to sit, stay, place* (see *pon-, posit-, sed-*) assess, obsess, possess

semi-   *half* (see *hemi-, demi-*) semicircle, semiconscious, semifinal

sen-   *old* (see *ger-, paleo-, vet-*) senate, senility, seignior

sens-   *to think, know, sense* (see *sci-, sent-, cog-, gnos-, wit-*) sensory, sensible, insensitive

sent-   *to think, know, sense* (see *sci-, sens-, cog-, gnos- wit-*) sentiment, sentinel, sentry

sept-   *seven* (see *hepta-*) September, septet, septennial

sequ-   *to follow* (see *sec-*) sequence, consequential, obsequious

sex-   *six* (see *hexa-*) sextet, siesta, sextant

-ship   *state or quality of* (see *-ry, -hood, -ness, -age, -ity, -cy, -ance, -ence, -ia*) friendship, partnership, fellowship

simul-   *same* (see *homo-*) simultaneity, similarity, facsimile, assimilate

sol-   (1) *one* (see *uni-, mono-*) sole, soliloquy, solo

sol-   (2) *sun* (see *helio-*) solstice, solarium

solut-   *to loosen* (see *solv-*) resolution, absolute, soluble

solv-   *to loosen* (see *solut-*) solve, resolve

soma-   *body, flesh* (see *carn-, corp-*) somatic, chromosome, somatogenic

-some   *resembling* (see *-like, -ly, -ish, -old*) handsome, lithesome, lonesome, burdensome, worrisome

somn-   *sleep* (see *dorm-, sopor-, hypno-, morph-, com-*) somnolent, somnambulism, somniferous

son-   *hearing, sound* (see *phon-, aud-, acou-*) sonic, dissonant, resonance, unison

soph-   *wise* (see *sag-*) sophomore, philosophy, sophist

sopor- *sleep* (see *dorm-, somn-, hypno-, morph-, com-*) soporific

soror- *sister* sororicide, sororal

spec- *to look, see* (see *vid-, vis-, scop-, scrut-;* variant form *spic-*) spectacle, conspicuous, inspector, perspicacity

sper- *hope* desperate, prosperous, desperado

spir- *breath, life* inspiration, spirit, expire, perspire

stab- *to stand* (see *stat-*) stability, stable, establish

stat- *to stand* (see *stab-;* variant form *stit-*) status, static, constitution

stead- *place* (see *loc-, top-*) steadfast, steady, bedstead, instead

stell- *star* (see *astr-*) stellar, stellate, Estelle

stig- *to mark* (variant forms *sting-, stinct-*) distinctive, instinct, stigma

strict- *to bind* (see *string-*) constrict, stricture, district

string- *to bind* (see *strict-*) astringent, constrain, prestige

stroph- *to turn* (see *vert-, rot-*) apostrophe, strophe, strobe

struct- *to build* destruction, structure, instruction, obstruct

sub- *under, below* (see *hypo-, infra-;* variant form *subter-*) subatomic, subzero, substandard

sui- *self* (see *auto-*) sui generis, suicide

sult- *to jump* (see *sault-, sal-*) result, exult, desultory

sum- *to use* sumptuous, assume, presume

super- *above, over* (see *hyper-;* variant forms *supr-, sur-*) supersonic, supervision, superior, survive

syn- *with, together* (see *con-, com-;* variant form *sym-*) sympathy, synthetic, symmetrical

T

tac-   *silent* (variant form *tic-*) taciturn, reticent

tact-   *to touch, feel* (see *tang-*) tactile, intact

tain-   *to hold* (see *ten-*) container, maintain, sustain

tang-   *to touch, feel* (see *tact-*) tangent, tangential

tard-   *slow* retard, tardigrade

techni-   *skill, craft* technical, technology, architect

tele-   *far* telekinesis, telephone, television, telemetric

tempor-   *time* (see *chron-*) extemporaneous, contemporary, temporal, temporize

ten-   (1) *to hold* (see *tain-*; variant form *tin-*) tenacious, retention, lieutenant, abstinence

ten-   (2) *to stretch* (variant form *tend-*) intensify, distend, detente, extenuate

term-   *end* (see *fin-*) terminal, exterminate, determine

terr-   *earth* (see *geo-*) terrain, terrarium, terrace

tetra-   *four* (see *quad-*) tetrahedron, tetrameter, tetragon

thana-   *death* (see *mort-, mori-*) thanatophobia

theo-   *God* (see *deo-*) theology, atheist, monotheism

therm-   *heat* thermal, thermometer, thermodynamics

-tion   *act or quality of* (see *-ism, -ation, -ure, -ment, -acy, -itude*) diction, action, participation

top-   *place* (see *loc-, stead-*) topical, ectopic, isotope, topography

tors-   *to twist* (see *tort-*) distorsion, extorsion

tort-   *to twist* (see *tors-*) tortuous, torture, distort

tract- *to pull* tractor, extract, detract, tractable

trans- *through, across* (see *dia-, per-*; variant form *tra-*) transport, translucent, trajectory

tri- *three* triple, trio, trivia, tripod, trident, trigonometry

tru- *faith* (see *fid-*) truth, betrothed, truce

tui- *to teach* (see *doc-, tut-*) tuition, intuit

turb- *to whirl, spin* (see *gyr-*) disturbance, perturb, turbine

tut- *to teach* (see *doc-, tui-*) tutelage, tutorial

U

ultim- *last* ultimate, penultimate

ultra- *beyond* (see *extra- meta-, para-*) ultramarine, ultramodern, outrage

umbr- *shadow* umbrage, adumbrate

un- *not* (see *non-, a-, an-, in-*) unkind, undone, unhappy

uni- *one* (see *mono-, sol-*) unity, universal, uniform

-ure *act or quality of* (see *-ism, -ation, -tion, -ment, -acy, -itude*) tenure, rupture, departure

V

vac- *empty* vacuous, evacuate, vacation

vali- *strong* (see *fort-*) valor, value, valid, equivalent

ven- *to come* (variant form *vance-*) adventure, convene, revenue, intervene, advance

vent- *wind* vent, ventilate

ver- *true* aver, verify, verdict

verb- *word* verbal, adverbial, verbiage

verg- *to tend toward* verging, divergent

vert-   *to turn* (see *strophe-, rot-;* variant form *vers-*) advertise, versatile, avert

vet-   *old* (see *ger-, paleo-, sen-*) inveterate, veterinary

via-   *road* trivial, deviate, voyage

vict-   *to conquer* (see *vinc-*) conviction, evict, victor

vid-   *to look, see* (see *vis-, spec-, scop-, scrut-*) evident, provide, videocamera

vinc-   *to conquer* (see *vict-;* variant form *vanqu-*) evince, vincible, convince, vanquish

vir-   *man* (see *anthr-, homo-*) virtue, triumvirate

vis-   *to look, see* (see *spec-, vid-, scop-, scrut-*) invisible, vision, revise

vit-   *life* (see *viv-, zoo-, bio-*) vital, vitamin, revitalize

viv-   *life* (see *vit-, zoo-, bio-*) convivial, revive, vivid

voc-   *to speak, talk, say* (see *dic-, loqu-, loc-, cit-*) vocation, vocal, vociferous

vol-   *to wish* volition, benevolent, malevolence, volunteer

volut-   *to roll* (see *volv-*) evolution, volute, vault

volv-   *to roll* (see *volut-*) revolve, volume, evolve

vor-   *to eat* carnivore, herbivore, omnivorous, voracious

W

well-   *good, well* (see *bene-, bon-, eu-*) wellborn, welcome, well-loved

wit-   *to know* (see *cogn-, sci-, sent-, sens-, gnos-;* variant form *wis-*) witness, witty, wisdom

with-   *against* (see *anti-, contra-, counter-, ob-*) withhold, withdraw

Z

zoo-   *life* (see *viv-, vit-, bio-*) zoologist, protozoan, zoo

Challenge 1

	SPEC, SPIC	JECT	DUC(T)	MIT, MIS	POS, PON	FER	SCRIB, SCRIP	CLAUS, CLOS, CLUD
AB		abject	abduct					
AD	aspect	adjective	adduce	admit		afferent	ascribe	
CON	conspicuous	conjecture	conduct	commit	compose	confer	conscript	conclude
DE	despicable	dejected	deduce	demise	depose	defer	describe	
E(X)	expect	eject	educe	emit	expose	efferent		exclude
IN	inspect	inject	induce		impose	infer	inscribe	include
INTER		interject		intermission	interpose	interfere		
INTRO	introspect	introjection	introduce	intromit				
OB		object		omit	oppose	offer		occlude
PER	perspective			permit				
PRE				premise	preposition	prefer	prescribe	preclude
PRO	prospect	project	produce	promise	propose	proffer	proscribe	
RE	respect	reject	reduce	remit	repose	refer		reclude
SUB	suspect	subject	subdue	submit	suppose	suffer	subscribe	
TRANS		trajectory	transduce	transmit	transpose	transfer	transcribe	

Challenge 2

ROOT ELEMENT: *turb* MEANING: whirl, spin CLUSTER: disturb, perturb

Prefix Meaning	Verb	Verbals (*ing, ed*)	Adjective (*ive, ial, ose, able, etc.*)	Adverb (*ly*)	Concrete Noun (*er, or, ar, ist, etc.*)	Abstract Noun (*ion, ship, ism, hood, etc.*)
poorly, bad	disturb	disturbing, disturbed	disturbable	disturbingly		disturbance
through	perturb	perturbing, perturbed	perturbable	perturbingly		perturbation

ROOT ELEMENT: *flect* MEANING: bend CLUSTER: deflect, reflect, inflect

Prefix Meaning	Verb	Verbals (*ing, ed*)	Adjective (*ive, ial, ose, able, etc.*)	Adverb (*ly*)	Concrete Noun (*er, or, ar, ist, etc.*)	Abstract Noun (*ion, ship, ism, hood, etc.*)
down	deflect	deflecting, deflected	deflectable			deflection
back again	reflect	reflecting, reflected	reflective	reflectively	reflector	reflection
in, into	inflect	inflecting, inflected	inflective			inflection

ROOT ELEMENT: *jac, jec* MEANING: throw CLUSTER: eject, reject, deject, inject, project

Prefix Meaning	Verb	Verbals (*ing, ed*)	Adjective (*ive, ial, ose, able, etc.*)	Adverb (*ly*)	Concrete Noun (*er, or, ar, ist, etc.*)	Abstract Noun (*ion, ship, ism, hood, etc.*)
out of	eject	ejecting, ejected	ejectable		ejector	ejection
back again	reject	rejecting, rejected	rejectable	rejectingly	rejector	rejection
down	deject	dejecting, dejected		dejectedly		dejection
in, into	inject	injecting, injected	injectable		injector	injection
before, forward	project	projecting, projected	projectable		projector, projectionist	projection

Challenge 4

		Hidden Elements		
		prefix	+	*word element*
1.	allusion	ad	+	lud
2.	suffuse	sub	+	fund
3.	occlusion	ob	+	clud
4.	irruption	in	+	rupt
5.	corrosive	con	+	rod
6.	effusive	ex	+	fund
7.	assimilate	ad	+	simil
8.	colloquial	con	+	loqu
9.	succumb	sub	+	cumb
10.	offer	ob	+	fer

Challenge 5

1. h
2. j
3. f
4. i
5. e
6. c
7. d
8. a
9. b
10. g

Challenge 6

1. d
2. h
3. f
4. c
5. b
6. i
7. g
8. e
9. a
10. j

Challenge 7

1. e
2. c
3. i
4. b
5. f
6. d
7. g
8. j
9. a
10. h

Challenge 8

1. i
2. g
3. f
4. b
5. j
6. h
7. e
8. d
9. a
10. c

Challenge 9

	Word	Prefix		Root(s)		Suffix	Part of Speech
1.	peripatetic	peri	+	patet	+	ic	adjective
2.	impeccable	im	+	pecc	+	able	adjective
3.	exculpate	ex	+	culp	+	ate	verb
4.	invincible	in	+	vinc	+	ible	adjective
5.	antagonist	ant(i)	+	agon	+	ist	noun
6.	heliocentric			helio, centr	+	ic	adjective
7.	celerity			celer	+	ity	noun
8.	misanthropic	mis	+	anthrop	+	ic	adjective
9.	proclivity	pro	+	cliv	+	ity	noun
10.	bellicose			belli(c)	+	ose	adjective

1.	peripatetic	walking all around; everywhere
2.	impeccable	without sin; faultless
3.	exculpate	to free from blame
4.	invincible	not able to be conquered
5.	antagonist	one who struggles against; adversary
6.	heliocentric	centered around the sun
7.	celerity	swiftness
8.	misanthropic	not liking people
9.	proclivity	a leaning towards; tendency
10.	bellicose	warlike

Challenge 10

	Word	Prefix Meaning	New Word (Example)
1.	*fore*tell	before	forewarning
2.	*pre*monition	before	prefix
3.	*ante*bellum	before	antedate
4.	*pro*rate	before, toward	protracted
5.	*post*pone	after	postgraduate
6.	*con*vocation	with, together	convivial
7.	*sym*pathy	with, together	symphony
8.	*anti*pathy	against	antibiotic
9.	*ob*struct	against	objection
10.	*contra*dict	against	contrary
11.	*counter*mand	against	counterproductive
12.	*with*hold	against	withstand

13.	*ab*solve	away, from	abstain
14.	*apo*logy	away, from	apocryphal
15.	*ad*vent	to, toward	adhere
16.	*hyper*kinetic	above, high	hypertension
17.	*super*sonic	above, high	supersensitive
18.	*hypo*dermic	below, low, under	hypoglycemia
19.	*sub*marine	below, low, under	substandard
20.	*sur*name	below, under	surrogate
21.	*infra*red	below, under	infrastructure
22.	*in*hibit	within, in	inclination
23.	*intra*mural	within, in	intravenous
24.	*endo*morphic	within, in	endocarditis

Challenge 11

	Word	**Word Element Meaning**	**New Word (Example)**
1.	pre*moni*tion	to warn, advise	admonish
2.	ante*bell*um	war	rebellion
3.	post*pone*	to place, position	deposit
4.	con*voc*ation	to call	evoke
5.	sym*pathy*	feelings, emotion	antipathy
6.	ob*struct*	to build	constructive
7.	contra*dict*	to speak, talk, say	dictionary
8.	ab*solve*	to loosen	dissolve
9.	apo*logy*	study, words	psychology
10.	ad*vent*	to come	circumvent
11.	hyper*kinetic*	motion	cinematic
12.	super*sonic*	sound	resonance
13.	hypo*dermic*	skin	dermatitis
14.	sub*marine*	sea	maritime
15.	subter*fuge*	to flee	refuge
16.	in*hibit*	to hold in	exhibit
17.	intra*mural*	wall	immure
18.	endo*morphic*	shape, form	metamorphosis
19.	en*demic*	people	democracy
20.	extra*terre*strial	earth	terrace

Challenge 12

1. h
2. e
3. g
4. j
5. c
6. i
7. d
8. a
9. b
10. f

Challenge 13

1. e
2. g
3. h
4. i
5. b
6. j
7. a
8. d
9. f
10. c

Challenge 14

1. f
2. c
3. j
4. i
5. g
6. e
7. d
8. a
9. h
10. b

Challenge 15

1. f
2. h
3. e
4. a
5. j
6. g
7. i
8. c
9. d
10. b

Challenge 16

1. f
2. g
3. a
4. j
5. c
6. b
7. i
8. e
9. d
10. h

Challenge 17

1. g
2. f
3. h
4. i
5. j
6. b
7. a
8. c
9. e
10. d

Challenge 18

1. h
2. g
3. i
4. f
5. j
6. b
7. a
8. d
9. e
10. c

Challenge 19

1. g
2. f
3. h
4. i
5. b
6. a
7. j
8. d
9. c
10. e

Challenge 20

1. murder of a king   regicide
2. to make by hand   manufacture
3. a warning against   admonition
4. pushing back   repel
5. to drag forward   protract
6. correct opinion   orthodox
7. light writing   photography

8. book lover   bibliophile
9. secret writing   cryptogram
10. fireworks   pyrotechnics
11. having to do with body and mind   psychosomatic
12. one who struggles against   antagonist
13. speech given before   prologue
14. state of not remembering   amnesia
15. without form or shape   amorphous

Challenge 21	Challenge 22	Challenge 23	Challenge 24
1. e	1. b	1. g	1. g
2. h	2. e	2. e	2. i
3. i	3. h	3. f	3. a
4. b	4. f	4. h	4. d
5. g	5. j	5. j	5. h
6. c	6. d	6. a	6. e
7. j	7. i	7. b	7. b
8. a	8. c	8. i	8. j
9. f	9. a	9. d	9. c
10. d	10. g	10. c	10. f

Challenge 25	Challenge 26	Challenge 27	Challenge 28
1. b	1. c	1. h	1. b
2. g	2. i	2. e	2. g
3. j	3. j	3. b	3. a
4. f	4. f	4. j	4. j
5. i	5. b	5. f	5. c
6. c	6. e	6. c	6. i
7. e	7. h	7. i	7. e
8. h	8. a	8. a	8. h
9. a	9. g	9. g	9. f
10. d	10. d	10. d	10. d

Challenge 29

1. a
2. d
3. d
4. c
5. d
6. d
7. b
8. a
9. b
10. d

Challenge 30

1. a
2. a
3. b
4. d
5. c
6. a
7. c
8. b
9. c
10. b

Challenge 31

1. b
2. c
3. a
4. c
5. b
6. a
7. b
8. a
9. c
10. b

Challenge 32

1. d
2. a
3. a
4. d
5. b
6. d
7. b
8. d
9. c
10. a

Challenge 33

1. b
2. c
3. a
4. b
5. d
6. b
7. c
8. d
9. a
10. b

Challenge 34

1. d
2. d
3. b
4. c
5. a
6. b
7. d
8. b
9. b
10. a

Challenge 35

1. e
2. g
3. f
4. b
5. i
6. c
7. h
8. j
9. a
10. d

Challenge 36

1. Sunday — k
2. Monday — n
3. Tuesday — f
4. Wednesday — r
5. Thursday — j
6. Friday — o
7. Saturday — c
8. January — i
9. February — s
10. March — p
11. April — g
12. May — q
13. June — e
14. July — l
15. August — a
16. September — h
17. October — t
18. November — m
19. December — b
20. Easter — d

Challenge 37

1. f
2. l
3. i
4. j
5. e
6. k
7. q
8. c
9. o
10. p
11. t
12. r
13. a
14. g
15. h
16. b
17. m
18. n
19. d
20. s

Challenge 38

1.	tycoon	m.	Japanese
2.	ketchup	n.	Chinese
3.	taboo	a.	Polynesian
4.	alcohol	l.	Arabic
5.	woodchuck	d.	Amerindian
6.	whiskey	k.	Gaelic
7.	boondocks	j.	Filipino
8.	umbrella	e.	Italian
9.	freight	b.	Dutch
10.	penguin	f.	Welsh
11.	cinnamon	h.	Hebrew
12.	coach	i.	Hungarian
13.	veranda	g.	Portuguese
14.	seersucker	c.	Hindi

Challenge 39

1. h
2. e
3. f
4. i
5. g
6. b
7. a
8. c
9. j
10. d

Challenge 40

1. j
2. f
3. g
4. i
5. b
6. c
7. a
8. d
9. e
10. h

Challenge 41

1. c
2. e
3. h
4. a
5. i
6. j
7. d
8. b
9. f
10. g

Challenge 42

1. g
2. c
3. f
4. a
5. h
6. i
7. d
8. j
9. b
10. e

Challenge 43

1. h   11. a
2. j   12. o
3. c   13. f
4. e   14. m
5. i   15. l
6. k
7. d
8. b
9. n
10. g

Challenge 44

1. f
2. i
3. g
4. a
5. c
6. h
7. j
8. e
9. b
10. d

Challenge 45

1. d
2. b
3. c
4. d
5. b
6. a
7. c
8. b
9. d
10. b

Challenge 46

1. c
2. b
3. a
4. b
5. a
6. d
7. b
8. d
9. a
10. c

Challenge 47

1. b
2. b
3. b
4. d
5. a
6. d
7. a
8. c
9. c
10. b

Challenge 48

1. d
2. d
3. d
4. d
5. c
6. c
7. d
8. a
9. b
10. a

Challenge 49

1. c
2. c
3. a
4. c
5. a
6. c
7. d
8. b
9. c
10. d

Challenge 50

1. a
2. d
3. d
4. a
5. a
6. d
7. a
8. a
9. c
10. d

Challenge 51

1. a
2. b
3. a
4. b
5. b
6. c
7. c
8. b
9. d
10. d

Challenge 52

1. b
2. c
3. a
4. c
5. a
6. a
7. b
8. b
9. d
10. c

Challenge 53

1. torturous . . . tortuous
2. reluctant . . . reticent
3. discreet . . . discrete
4. stationery . . . stationary
5. loathe . . . loath
6. incredulous . . . incredible
7. aggravate . . . irritate
8. laid . . . lay
9. capacity . . . ability
10. anticipate . . . expect

Challenge 54

1.	awake	awoke	have awoken
2.	bid	bade	have bidden
3.	bind	bound	have bound
4.	bite	bit	have bitten
5.	blow	blew	have blown
6.	break	broke	have broken
7.	cleave	clove	have cloven
8.	dive	dove	have dived
9.	draw	drew	have drawn
10.	fly	flew	have flown
11.	forsake	forsook	have forsaken
12.	lie	laid	have laid
13.	leave	left	have left
14.	lay	lay	have lain
15.	melt	melted	have melted
16.	mow	mowed	have mown
17.	rise	rose	have risen
18.	shave	shaved	have shaven
19.	slay	slew	have slain
20.	strike	struck	have stricken
21.	swear	swore	have sworn
22.	swell	swelled	have swollen
23.	tear	tore	have torn
24.	tread	trod	have trodden

Challenge 55

1. mothers-in-law
2. sargeants-at-arms
3. men-of-war
4. courts-martial
5. chiefs-of-staff
6. rights-of-way
7. attorneys-general
8. aides-de-camp
9. vice-presidents
10. sons-in-law

Challenge 56

Irregular Plurals	*Collective Nouns*
child/children	committee
louse/lice	class
goose/geese	team
brother/brethren	crew
	crowd
	army

Challenge 57

1. government
2. correct
3. guerilla
4. minuscule
5. judgment
6. chamois
7. correct
8. correct
9. philistine
10. correct

Nouns with no Singular	*Nouns with no Plural*
trousers	cattle
scissors	wheat
billiards	courage
shears	deer
pliers	sheep

Challenge 58

1. supersede
2. intercede
3. accede
4. exceed
5. recede
6. concede
7. proceed
8. secede
9. precede
10. succeed

Challenge 59

	Verb	Noun	Adjective
1.	admire	admiration	admirable
2.	admit	admission	admissible
3.	exhaust	exhaustion	exhaustible
4.	inflame	inflammation	inflammable
5.	convert	conversion	convertible
6.	imagine	imagination	imaginable
7.	immerse	immersion	immersible
8.	permit	permission	permissible
9.	adore	adoration	adorable
10.	comprehend	comprehension	comprehensible

Challenge 60

1.	a	11.	b
2.	a	12.	d
3.	c	13.	b
4.	b	14.	b
5.	c	15.	d
6.	a		
7.	d		
8.	b		
9.	a		
10.	b		

Challenge 61

1.	d	10.	d
2.	b	11.	c
3.	d	12.	b
4.	c	13.	c
5.	c	14.	d
6.	b	15.	d
7.	c		
8.	a		
9.	b		

Challenge 62

1.	c	11.	a
2.	d	12.	d
3.	a	13.	d
4.	d	14.	d
5.	d	15.	c
6.	b		
7.	b		
8.	a		
9.	b		
10.	c		

Challenge 63

1.	e	11.	e
2.	a	12.	c
3.	b	13.	a
4.	b	14.	a
5.	b	15.	a
6.	c		
7.	c		
8.	a		
9.	b		
10.	d		

Challenge 64

1.	b	10.	b
2.	c	11.	c
3.	a	12.	d
4.	a	13.	c
5.	d	14.	c
6.	d	15.	b
7.	c		
8.	a		
9.	d		

Challenge 65

1.	c	11.	b
2.	d	12.	b
3.	d	13.	b
4.	d	14.	d
5.	a	15.	b
6.	d		
7.	c		
8.	b		
9.	a		
10.	b		

Challenge 66

1.	e	11.	e
2.	b	12.	a
3.	b	13.	b
4.	d	14.	a
5.	c	15.	c
6.	d		
7.	a		
8.	b		
9.	c		
10.	d		

Challenge 67

1.	a	11.	c
2.	c	12.	a
3.	d	13.	c
4.	b	14.	a
5.	d	15.	c
6.	b	16.	a
7.	d	17.	c
8.	b	18.	a
9.	d	19.	c
10.	b	20.	a

Challenge 68

1.	c	11.	b
2.	c	12.	c
3.	a	13.	d
4.	c	14.	d
5.	a	15.	a
6.	c	16.	a
7.	a	17.	c
8.	c	18.	d
9.	a	19.	a
10.	c	20.	d

Challenge 69

1. d	11. b
2. d	12. d
3. d	13. b
4. b	14. b
5. d	15. d
6. b	16. b
7. d	17. d
8. b	18. b
9. d	19. c
10. b	20. a

Challenge 70

1. d	11. d
2. a	12. d
3. c	13. b
4. d	14. d
5. c	15. b
6. d	16. d
7. b	17. b
8. d	18. d
9. b	19. b
10. d	20. d

Challenge 71

1. a	11. c
2. c	12. a
3. b	13. c
4. d	14. a
5. b	15. c
6. c	16. a
7. a	17. d
8. d	18. b
9. a	19. d
10. a	20. b

Challenge 72

1. c	11. c
2. a	12. a
3. c	13. c
4. a	14. a
5. c	15. c
6. a	16. a
7. c	17. c
8. a	18. a
9. c	19. c
10. a	20. a

Challenge 73

1. a	11. c
2. c	12. a
3. c	13. c
4. a	14. a
5. c	15. c
6. a	16. a
7. c	17. c
8. a	18. a
9. c	19. c
10. a	20. a

Challenge 74

1. b	11. d
2. d	12. b
3. b	13. d
4. d	14. b
5. b	15. d
6. c	16. c
7. d	17. a
8. b	18. c
9. d	19. a
10. b	20. c

Challenge 75

1. c	11. a
2. a	12. c
3. c	13. a
4. a	14. c
5. a	15. a
6. c	16. d
7. a	17. b
8. c	18. d
9. a	19. b
10. c	20. d

Try these fine references from America's best-selling family of dictionaries.

Available at fine bookstores everywhere.

Webster's New World Dictionary®
Third College Edition

Webster's New World™ Thesaurus
New Revised Edition

Webster's New World™
Compact Dictionary
of American English

Webster's New World™
Pocket Dictionary

Webster's New World™
Power Vocabulary

Webster's New World™
Speller/Divider

Webster's New World™
Misspeller's Dictionary

Webster's New World™
Compact School and Office Dictionary

PRENTICE HALL

BOOKS FOR COLLEGE-BOUND STUDENTS

COLLEGE ENTRANCE

ACT: American College Testing Program
ACT Cram Course
ACT SuperCourse
AP American History
AP Biology
AP Chemistry
AP Computer Science
AP English Composition and Literature
AP European History
AP Mathematics
College Board Achievement Test
 in Mathematics: Level I
College Board Achievement Test
 in Mathematics: Level II
College Board Achievement Test in Spanish
College Board Achievement Tests SuperCourse
English Workbook for the New ACT
Mathematics Workbook for the New ACT
Nursing School Entrance Examinations
PCAT: Pharmacy College Admissions Test
Preparation for the SAT: Scholastic Aptitude Test
SAT Cram Course
SAT Math Workbook
SAT SuperCourse
SAT Verbal Workbook
SAT-II Writing
TOEFL: Test of English as a Foreign Language
TOEFL Grammar Workbook
TOEFL Reading and Vocabulary Workbook
TOEFL Skills for Top Scores
TOEFL SuperCourse

COLLEGE GUIDES

The American Film Institute Guide to College Courses
 in Film and Television
College Applications and Essays

College Financial Aid
College Survival
Lovejoy's College Guide
The Performing Arts Major's College Guide
The Right College
The Transfer Student's Guide

STUDY AIDS

Associated Press Guide to News Writing
Consumer and Business Mathematics
College Time Tracker
Essential English Composition for College-Bound
 Students
Essential Math for College-Bound Students
Essential Vocabulary for College-Bound
 Students
High School Time Tracker
How to Develop and Write a Research Paper
How to Read and Interpret Poetry
How to Read and Write about Drama
How to Read and Write about Fiction
How to Solve Algebra Word Problems
How to Write Book Reports
How to Write Poetry
How to Write Short Stories
How to Write Themes and Essays
How to Write a Thesis
1001 Ideas for Science Projects
Reading Lists for College-Bound Students
10,000 Ideas for Term Papers, Projects, Reports,
 and Speeches
Triple Your Reading Speed
Webster's New World™ Power Vocabulary
Webster's New World™ Student Writing
 Handbook

AVAILABLE AT BOOKSTORES EVERYWHERE

PRENTICE HALL